TIMELY LESSONS FROM THE BOOK OF EXODUS

TIMELY LESSONS FROM THE BOOK OF

EXODUS

JIM PAUL

GOSPEL FOLIO PRESS
www.gospelfolio.com

TIMELY LESSONS FROM THE BOOK OF EXODUS
by Jim Paul

Published by
GOSPEL FOLIO PRESS
304 Killaly St. W.
Port Colborne, ON, Canada L3K 6A6
1-800-952-2382
www.gospelfolio.com

Scripture taken from the Authorized King James Version, unless otherwise noted.

ISBN 1-897117-40-X

Cover design by Rachel Brooks

Printed in the United States of America.

Contents

Preface 7
Introduction 9

CHAPTER 1
A Family in Egypt 11

CHAPTER 2
God's Promises Remembered 15

CHAPTER 3
God's Purpose Revealed 19

CHAPTER 4
God's Presence Assured 23

CHAPTER 5
An Unforgettable Night 29

CHAPTER 6
Ready for the Journey 37

CHAPTER 7
The Journey Begins 41

CHAPTER 8
A Change of Heart 45

CHAPTER 9
A Song to Sing 51

CHAPTER 10
New Experiences in the Way 57

CHAPTER 11
Bread from Heaven.. 63

CHAPTER 12
Water from the Rock 69

CHAPTER 13
The Enemy Attacks 73

CHAPTER 14
The Law was Given 79

CHAPTER 15
God's Dwelling Place 85

CHAPTER 16
Final Comments 89

PREFACE

When I was thirteen years old, my Bible class teacher, John Miller, first introduced me to the book of Exodus. John later became a dear friend and is now with the Lord. The memory of those days still linger—memories of when he thrilled and challenged the hearts of his young students. In recent years, reading over this exciting subject once again has brought invaluable lessons for the pilgrim way. The history of events that took place is undisputed. *"These things happened unto them for ensamples: and they are written for our admonition"* (1 Cor. 10:11). It is wonderful to think that God allowed the record of these exodus experiences to be preserved for us. Since this is so, we ought to pay particular attention to this book of Exodus and to its teaching. The lessons to be learned will be highlighted through spending time in the Word of God. I encourage the reader to get acquainted with this unique and interesting book of the Bible by careful reading. The book of Exodus lays a solid foundation for understanding what it means to be associated with God's people. God, in a beautiful way, presents to us a pattern in picture form, which later becomes principles through New Testament revelation. The church today is not a substitute for Israel but is a separate entity in itself. Nevertheless, the Church of God can learn much from Israel's experiences. It is my prayer that you will, through these meditations, give the book of Exodus your earnest consideration. To the seasoned traveler, may it be spiritual refreshment in familiar territory. For the new or young believer in Christ, may it open a vast storehouse of good things to be possessed and enjoyed! No matter how often this journey is taken with the children of Israel there will be new paths to discover and new truths to learn.

—Jim Paterson Paul

INTRODUCTION

The book of Exodus is a classic in world history. However, as a textbook of world history, it also holds for its readers, both young and old, a fascinating insight into God's dealings with mankind. Each chapter is full of intrigue, charm, wonder, and challenge. Vitally important lessons are stamped upon each fascinating event bringing the careful reader to a deeper understanding of spiritual values and truths! There are three main divisions to the book—divisions which parallel the experiences of the people of God.

GOD DELIVERS HIS PEOPLE: Chapters 1-12

The book opens with a look at Jacob's posterity. The reader is reminded of the blessings received by the children of Israel through their saviour, Joseph, who although despised by his brethren was a special son to his father. Joseph was wrongfully treated as a servant and was cast into prison. But later he comes to a place of exaltation as saviour and lord in Egypt. However, with the passing of time, Joseph died, as did his brethren and all of that generation (Ex. 1:6). *"Now there arose a new king over Egypt, who did not know Joseph"* (1:8). When this new pharaoh takes his place as ruler of Egypt, circumstances change radically for the people of God. It is at this low point in their national history that God steps in to reveal his amazing plan to deliver them out of their bondage and sorrow.

GOD DIRECTS HIS PEOPLE: Chapters 13-24

The full impact of God's dealings with Pharaoh and Egypt reached its climax when, *"There was not a house where there was not one dead"* (Ex. 12:30). This final blow in one of the darkest nights of Egyptian history brought on them defeat and disaster. What a revelation to Israel, and to us, of God's love to His people, of God's power, and His desire and authority to redeem them! What a demonstration to Israel of the mighty hand of God at work in setting them free! This great nation was not only delivered from a powerful enemy but was prepared to journey to the land God had promised them. Not only did He promise them the land, but He also promised to go with them every step of the way. Let's enjoy these experiences, so rich in instruction and grace, which they encountered on their journey forward!

GOD DWELLS IN THE MIDST OF HIS PEOPLE: Chapters 25-40

We now come to the section in which God's people are brought to the place He desired them to be. Now they are separated from Egypt and in the wilderness, He will be their God and they will be His people. They are given an opportunity to *"make Me a sanctuary, that I may dwell among them"* (Ex. 25:8).

What beautiful pictures and object lessons are presented in these chapters! They have been the subject of many books and the theme of many preachers. I pray this brief outline will give you a deeper desire to open your Bible and to follow through each stage. This book is in no way exhaustive, but it explores the edges of an immense gold mine of truth. Further careful and prayerful reading of the Word of God will yield rich rewards.

1

A FAMILY IN EGYPT

It is hard for us to imagine what it would have been like for the children of Israel to experience such a remarkable turn of events. The relatively calm and pleasant environment they had enjoyed under the care of Joseph, was gone. All of Joseph's generation had died. Now there was confronting them *"a new king over Egypt, who did not know Joseph"* (1:8). This Pharaoh assessed his situation and discovered that the children of Israel were multiplying and becoming stronger than the Egyptians. Human logic took over and he feared his authority and posterity were in grave danger. Of course, we realize that it was God who was at work effecting a remarkable plan to take His people out of Egypt. It is to this end that God brought in this new leader to accomplish this purpose. For the Scripture says about Pharaoh, *"For this very purpose I have raised you up, that I may show My power in you, and that My name may be declared in all the earth"* (Rom. 9:17). God has changed leaders in many other nations in order to fulfill His will, as well as to cause His people to prepare for a move. Egypt was not home for the Israelites, even though they were settled and content to stay there. It is a valuable exercise to look through Scripture and find the different times God worked in this way. One good example was when persecution came to the early church in Jerusalem. Many disciples had to scatter into other regions but this served rather to fulfill the great commission, *"Go into all the world and preach the gospel"* (Mark 16:15). God has frequently used opposition to unsettle believers so they would leave their homes and serve Him elsewhere. There is a grave danger in settling down to a life of ease and apathy. We should always be in the forefront of responsibility and service, whether at home or abroad.

The plight of God's people under Egyptian bondage seemed to be hopeless. They had a cruel master who forced them to carry heavy burdens and who enslaved them to his every demand. What a picture this is of the enemy, Satan himself. We know he has many titles, each one showing something of his evil character. The attitude of Pharaoh clearly sums it up when he said, *"Who is the LORD, that I should obey His voice to let Israel go? I do not know the LORD, nor will I let Israel go"* (Ex. 5:2). This is open defiance and rebellion against the God of Heaven. Notice where this all stems from. It comes from the heart of Lucifer, the greatest and most beautiful angel God created. He said,

> *"I will ascend into heaven,*
> *I will exalt my throne above the stars of God;*
> *I will also sit on the mount of the congregation*
> *On the farthest sides of the north;*
> *I will ascend above the heights of the clouds,*
> *I will be like the Most High"* (Isa. 14:13-14).

What arrogance! But it brought the severity of divine judgment upon him. From that moment on, he became the enemy of God and God's people. Satan was seeking the downfall of the human race. He accomplished this by deception, instilling into the heart of Eve the desire to be as God (Gen. 3:5).

Many examples show us something of Satan's deceptive character. The first great example is in the life of Pharaoh, lord of Egypt. Egypt speaks to us of the world system. In order to examine this more fully, look at what Scripture says in relation to it. When Lot looked over the well-watered plains of Sodom and Gomorrah he saw that it was *"like the land of Egypt"* (Gen. 13:10). Lot saw a land with great natural resources which tempted his heart to put up his tent there. This fertile plain had every thing to satisfy all his heart's desire. Very soon

Lot lost his pilgrim character for *"that righteous man, dwelling among them, tormented his righteous soul from day to day by seeing and hearing their lawless deeds"* (2 Pet. 2:8). What a challenge to us today! We are saved, but are we spending our time seeking satisfaction in temporal things and not living in the good of our Heavenly heritage?

Secondly, in Proverbs we are told of what the harlot said in seeking to attract the young man void of understanding *"I have spread my bed with tapestry, Colored coverings of Egyptian linen"* (7:16). This brings before us the seductive and immoral aspect of the world society we live in. *"With her flattering lips she seduced him … as an ox goes to the slaughter"* (7:21-22). How many lives have been broken, ruined and destroyed by yielding to the allurements of this sinful world. The deceptive work of Satan is often presented in attractive packages but the outcome is dangerous and deadly.

Thirdly, Isaiah 31:1 says,

> *Woe to those who go down to Egypt for help,*
> *And rely on horses,*
> *Who trust in chariots because they are many,*
> *And in horsemen because they are very strong,*
> *But who do not look to the Holy One of Israel,*
> *Nor seek the LORD!*

Here we see the great military power and might of Egypt, a place where many have put their confidence and trust! Isaiah warns us, *"the Egyptians are men, and not God; And their horses are flesh, and not spirit"* (v. 3). The teachings of secular humanism and new philosophies have deluded many into thinking that man is the master of his own destiny; all the strength he needs is inherent in himself. He has the power to do whatever he wants to do. King Solomon, one of the wisest of men says, *"There is a way that seems right to a man, But its end is the way of death"* (Prov. 16:25). Ultimately, all the hopes and dreams of man end in the grave. David says, *"It is better to trust in the LORD Than to put confidence in man"* (Ps. 118:8).

Finally, Acts 7:22 says, *"Moses was learned in all the wisdom of the Egyptians, and was mighty in words and deeds."* What a lesson for us today as we evaluate the wisdom of this world. 1 Corinthians 1:20 tells us *"God made foolish the wisdom of this world."* But intellectual men and women do not want to lower themselves to bring God into their thinking! What a great distance lies between the thoughts of God and the thoughts of men. Isaiah 55:9 says *"For as the heavens are higher than the earth, So are My ways higher than your ways, And My thoughts than your thoughts."* How we need, in the spiritual realm, to be careful not to interject our own thoughts and ideas. God has given us His Word which is sufficient to meet our every need. Moses, with all his learning, came to a point of decision one day, *"choosing rather to suffer affliction with the people of God than to enjoy the passing pleasures of sin, esteeming the reproach of Christ greater riches than the treasures in Egypt; for he looked to the reward"* (Heb. 11:25-26). What a momentous decision! This decision was going to cost him popularity, power, and wealth! Moses recognized that eternal things were more valuable than temporal things. He believed that suffering with the people of God would bring much greater joy than all the pleasures of sin, which would last for such a little time. So, in these few references, it is clear that Egypt speaks of the world. John exhorts us: *"Do not love the world or the things in the world"* (1 Jn. 2:15).

So here are God's people in Egypt, laden with heavy burdens, and their cry reaches heaven! The wonderful thing is *"God heard their groaning, and God remembered His covenant with Abraham, with Isaac, and with Jacob. And God looked upon the children of Israel, and God acknowledged them"* (Ex. 2:24-25). Now God was preparing to act in a mighty way, an unforgettable way, to bring about their wonderful deliverance.

2

GOD'S PROMISES REMEMBERED

It is good for us to remember that, although God's people were suffering, He was fully aware of all that was happening to them. Perhaps a believer today, passing through a difficult time, can take confidence in the fact that He knows all about it! Behind what is taking place, He is working out His wonderful purpose for His eternal glory. It is here we now turn to see the Sovereignty of God at work. In a unique and special way He moves in human affairs to fulfill His purposes in relation to his own people.

It all begins when a king arises who did not know Joseph. The blessings experienced because of Joseph are taken away from the children of Israel. Now they are being afflicted by this cruel monarch who has appointed masters over them to increase their burdens. However, the more afflictions were brought upon the people, the more they grew and multiplied. This has always been the case when God's people have been put through the fire of affliction. Instead of having a weakening and humiliating effect on them, affliction can bring a certain amount of confidence and strength. Pharaoh thought that if these people multiplied any more they would take over and his people would become their servants. So, he came up with a cruel plan to avert the pending disaster he was convinced Egypt was facing.

A KING'S CRUEL EDICT

Speaking to the Hebrew midwives, Pharaoh ordered that if a son were born he was to be killed, but if a daughter, she was allowed to live. Nevertheless, the midwives feared God and did not submit to the demand of the king. Their faithfulness to God under those trying circumstances ultimately gave them favor in the eyes of the King of kings. Because of this, the people kept on multiplying, becoming stronger in spite of the hostility against them. Pharaoh then bypassed the midwives and gave a strongly worded edict to all his people that every newborn Hebrew son had to be drowned in the river. We cannot imagine the tremendous distress and sorrow this caused. It would seem that at this point in time that their situation was utterly hopeless. Their cries were now ascending to the very heart of God. The wonderful thing is, He heard them! Now the time had come for Him to step in and to implement His own plan, to bring the downfall of this cruel monarch. The reason God was moved to act in this situation was that He remembered His covenant with Abraham, Isaac and Jacob. He was still the God of their fathers!

A SPECIAL SON BORN

Against this dark background of events and tremendous loss, there was working in the hearts of two parents a desire to save their child from this unthinkable fate. Courageously choosing to defy the King's command, they hid their newborn son. Realizing he was special to God, they hid him for three months until they could conceal him no longer. In the meantime, his mother made a basket from bulrushes. Placing him in it, she laid the basket in the river, the very place he should have been drowned at birth. Having done all she could, she left the rest with her God. What simple lessons we can learn from the experience of this dear mother. There are times in life when we are in anxious circumstances. It is then we too have to leave the matter with the Lord. Sure we have to do what we can, but then we must leave matters entirely with Him. So often, we don't take our concerns to the Lord, but instead we worry, fret and fear. Oh, that we might do what this mother did and *"Cast your burden on the LORD, And He shall sustain you"* (Ps. 55:22).

In the interests of their child the parents played a very important role. It is worth noting that the child's sister is hidden nearby keeping a watchful, caring eye upon her little brother. We give thanks to God for sisters who, at a distance from what is happening, have a spiritual caring interest in matters that relate to us. How many have interceded before the throne of grace, taking our deep concerns to the Lord in prayer. Many others who look on at a distance are yet involved in one way or another in seeing us through the difficult times. This dear sister was going to play a significant role in the lives of her brothers in the years ahead. How delightful that the New Testament reminds us of the events of this very important time in Israel's history. Stephen, in Acts 7:20, speaks of Moses' father as one who provided nourishment. The writer to the Hebrews on the other hand lays emphasis on the child's protection. Both parents feared God more than the king's commandment and their faith placed them in that notable company *"of whom the world was not worthy"* (Heb. 11:23).

A PRINCESS WHO HAD COMPASSION

In the course of events, the royal princess came down with her maidens to wash in the river. This could have been either part of her daily routine or just an occasional visit to this place. Whatever the case may be, it was the right time for her to come according to the providential ways of God. Once again we see how God can take the ordinary events of life and make them an extraordinary experience. Also, there was from the heavenly realm, a watchful eye upon this little, helpless child. God was going to bring about the child's salvation so that He could use him in a unique and wonderful way.

As the princess approached the riverbank she observed the basket among the reeds. Asking the maid to bring it to her, she opened the lid, and at that very moment the child began to cry. How amazing is the explicit timing of God's direction to move the very heart of the king's daughter. She immediately observed that this was a Hebrew child. But in spite of the edict of her father, she had compassion on him. From the place where he should have been drowned, he is now taken out—hence the meaning of his name, Moses. Now events are set in motion through which he eventually would be right in the palace of the king himself. The apostle Paul accurately exclaims in Romans 11:33 *"Oh, the depth of the riches both of the wisdom and knowledge of God! How unsearchable are His judgments and His ways past finding out!"*

It is interesting that Miriam was the one who suggested that the princess get a nurse for the child from the Hebrew women. Who better to care for Moses than his mother! We cannot underestimate the great contribution to Moses' life that his mother gave him. If a mother is reading this book, remember the great part you play in your children's spiritual welfare and development. In our western civilization, many have abandoned this God-given role of motherhood for a place in a Satanic-controlled, materialistic and self-centred world. How much hurt have children experienced because of this sad condition of our times!

A GROWING SON

The formative years of Moses' life were, without question, under the godly influence of his mother. She took him home and instilled in him the values of his God-given heritage. No doubt she would have much to teach him with regard to Abraham, Isaac and Jacob. There comes a time, however, when Moses is brought into the palace to be the Princess' son. I have often wondered what Pharaoh thought as he looked upon Moses knowing he ought to have been drowned. Here in the palace he *"was learned in all the wisdom of the Egyptians, and was mighty in words and deeds"* (Acts 7:22). He was a young man who literally had the world at his feet.

3

GOD'S PURPOSE REVEALED

It seems incredible that forty years passed with scarcely a word since this young son had been pulled out of the river. In all the early years of his experience Moses was not aware that God was preparing him to become a leader of His people. In our own spiritual growth we are often unaware of where this training will ultimately lead in the counsels of God! Every experience He brings us through, whether good or painful, builds character and brings fitness for His service.

Moses did not realize, while learning *"all the wisdom of the Egyptians"* (Acts 7:22), that God had other plans for his life. Here was a young man with the world at his feet—with power, riches, wisdom and all the other things that go along with it. One day Moses left the splendor of the palace and came to his brethren and his heart was moved as he saw their plight. A Hebrew slave was being beaten by an Egyptian. So Moses, thinking no one was around, slew the Egyptian and buried him in the sand. How often we think that when wrong actions are done, no one will ever know! However, whatever is done in secret will be made manifest. Maybe not at the immediate moment, but in due course, it will be brought to light. The very next day Moses was confronted about his actions when he came upon two Hebrews who were fighting one another. As Moses sought to intervene, the wrongdoer challenged him, *"Who made you a prince and a judge over us? Do you intend to kill me as you killed the Egyptian?"* (Ex. 2:14). This pierced the conscience of

Moses. He became afraid and fled into the desert. Sin always brings a troubled conscience, awakening fear in the heart. The easy way out was to run away from it all.

Many have lived lives like this—always on the run, never stopping to confess their sins and to seek God's forgiveness and peace. Remember our first parents in the Garden of Eden when they sinned! First, they tried to cover up their sin by making a garment of fig leaves, but this did not help. Then they were afraid, and hid themselves. In other words, they tried to run away from the situation, but this also did not work. It was only when they heard the voice of God speaking to them that they came out from their hiding.

God was now able to give them a true covering for their sin. A sacrifice was made, blood was shed, and an innocent victim died so that a covering of skin could be provided. This is a picture of the greater sacrifice that took place at Calvary. Here the sinless Saviour died for our sins, and provided the garment of His righteousness as a true covering for all our sin. To all who are running away from God because of sin the message is: stop running, and trust Jesus Christ as Saviour and Lord. Then you will know that true peace which He alone can bring. For those who have drifted away from the Lord because of sin, there is still a remedy. First John 1:9 says, *"If we confess our sins, He is faithful and just to forgive us our sins and to cleanse us from* ***all*** *unrighteousness."*

Looking back again on the events that were taking place in Egypt, there are some valuable things to consider. When the enemy attacks and opposition comes, we can expect similar problems to these. It is sad when God's people are fighting among themselves. Paul, in 1st Corinthians chapter 1, addressing the church at Corinth, exhorts that there be no divisions among them. He highlights the source of the problem. They were saying, *"'I am of Paul,' or 'I am of Apollos,' or 'I am of Cephas,' or 'I am of Christ'"* (v. 12). They were using various men as leaders of groups when these men were only **ministers through whom they believed**. Those servant leaders were not in competition with each other, but were a complement to each other in the work of God. There is always a great danger when men are put on a pedestal and we follow them. It is generally true that most divisions among the Lord's people are the result of personality clashes, and are not over teaching of the Word of God. Consider the beautiful words of the psalmist in Psalm 133:1-3:

> *Behold, how good and how pleasant it is*
> *For brethren to dwell together in unity!*
> *It is like the precious oil upon the head,*
> *Running down on the beard,*
> *The beard of Aaron,*
> *Running down on the edge of his garments.*
> *It is like the dew of Hermon,*
> *Descending upon the mountains of Zion;*
> *For there the LORD commanded the blessing—*
> *Life forevermore.*

Note the simple exhortation to two devoted sisters who laboured with Paul in the gospel *"to be of the same mind in the Lord"* (Phil. 4:2). In fact, to the whole assembly he writes, *"Fulfill my joy by being like-minded, having the same love, being of one accord, of one mind"* (2:2). There will always be conflicts which need to be resolved, but may the Lord give grace to bear and forbear bringing honour and glory to our Lord Jesus Christ. *"By this all will know that you are My disciples, if you have love for one another"* (John 13:35).

Coming back again to our "man on the run" it is interesting how a changed set of circumstances brought him into an entirely new role. God was going to further equip him for what lay ahead. He now moved from Egypt to dwell in the land of Midian. It is here that he sat down by a well and the seven daughters of Ruel, the priest of Midian, came with their father's flocks to draw water. The young women were challenged by shepherds who tried to drive them away from the well. Once again we see Moses entering into conflict as he stands up to defend the girls and the sheep. This is where we see his true shepherd heart taking over in defence of the flock. This man, who in a later day would lead the people of God as a mighty army, had the heart of a shepherd. We also remember David in this connection, as well as *"The good shepherd* [who] *gives His life for the sheep"* (John 10:11). Good leaders among God's people will rule, not with a rod of iron, but with a tender loving care for the flock of God. The defence of those flocks brought Moses to the household of Jethro where he was introduced as an Egyptian. Although a Hebrew, he was still wearing the princely garment of an Egyptian.

Already we have seen that Egypt speaks of the world. So we have here a picture of a believer who still shows characteristics of the world. As you read this today, what is your relationship to the world? How do others see you? Are you being identified with the Lord Jesus Christ, or are you no different from the world? The disciples were first called Christians at Antioch (Acts 11:26). It is here they were identified as being Christ's ones! Do others truly see we are associated with the Lord Jesus Christ? How beautiful the words in John 17:16, *"They are not of the world, just as I am not of the world."* James, in his epistle, reminds us, *"Do you not know that friendship with the world is enmity with God?"* (4:4). God does not expect us to be isolated from the world, but to be separate from its false ways!

4

GOD'S PRESENCE ASSURED

In the providential ways of God, Moses settled down to another 40 years of training. This time it was not in the palace with all its pomp and ceremony, but in a desert, taking care of flocks of sheep. It was during one of those ordinary days that he had a unique and remarkable experience. One day he caught sight of a bush that kept on burning but was not being consumed. Stephen, in referring to this scene, says that Moses *"marveled at the sight; and as he drew near to observe, the voice of the Lord came to him"* (Acts 7:31). The account given in Exodus says, *"Moses said, 'I will now turn aside and see this great sight, why the bush does not burn.'"* (Ex. 3:3). His quiet peaceful life in the desert was just about over, for God had other things for him to do. God spoke to him and called him twice by name. It must be a delight to God's heart when our ears are tuned to hear His voice and our hearts are receptive to reply, *"Here am I!"* (Ex. 3:4).

The question to each of us is then: Is my ear tuned to God speaking to me through His Word? Have I considered the cost of a surrendered heart and life to the will of God? Or is this just another story we like to read without any conviction to our souls? Perhaps this little book will stir you up to do what the Lord has laid upon your heart.

The Lord now says to Moses, *"Do not draw near this place. Take your sandals off your feet, for the place where you stand is holy ground"* (Ex. 3:5). The Lord was about to reveal some wonderful things to Moses and his immediate response was to hide his face for he was afraid to look upon God (3:6).There was now in him a deep reverential awe of God! This made him realize his own unworthiness and inability for the task before him. Joy must have filled Moses' heart when he heard God call Himself the father of Abraham, Isaac and Jacob! The patriarchs were the recipients of divine promises resulting in Jacob, whose name was changed to Israel, becoming the father of a great nation.

At this point in time the situation back in Egypt was desperate and the children of Israel looked like anything but a great nation! In fact, the Lord tells Moses *"I have surely seen the oppression of My people who are in Egypt, and have heard their cry because of their taskmasters; for I know their sorrows"* (Ex. 3:7). The compassionate eye of God was looking down. God heard their groaning and remembered His covenant with Abraham, Isaac and Jacob. The time had arrived for God to come down and deliver His people. An interesting dialogue follows between the Lord and Moses. The Lord unveiled His plan: *"Come now, therefore, and I will send you to Pharaoh, that you may bring the children of Israel out of Egypt"* (3:10). It must have struck a blow into Moses' heart at the very thought of returning and facing the mighty monarch of Egypt. This stupendous task forced him to take a look at himself and to reply, *"Who am I that I should go to Pharaoh, and that I should bring the children of Israel out of Egypt?"* (3:11). Isn't this a remarkable change from the young man who was going to sort out the problems all by himself in his own way. He now realized how utterly impossible it was to take on this great responsibility and he doubtfully questioned the Lord's choice of him.

Down through the centuries God has used His servants in remarkable ways when they recognized their own inadequacy and trusted Him totally for their strength. The real danger comes when we move along in the energy of the flesh and not in the power of the Holy Spirit of God. The words of Paul in the epistle to the Philippians 2:13 confirm this principle: *"For it is God who worketh in you both to will and to do of His good pleasure."* He puts His will in the heart, and then He gives the ability to accomplish His will for His own eternal glory. In chapter four of the same letter he says, *"I can do all things through Christ who strengtheneth me"* (4:13). Paul says again, *"We have such trust through Christ toward God. Not that we are sufficient of ourselves to think anything of ourselves, but our sufficiency is from God* (2 Cor. 3:4-5). Whatever the area of service God has laid upon your heart, He will provide all the resources necessary to accomplish His work.

Moses now has his ear tuned to the voice of God and his heart is in a right condition before God. The Lord gave him a wonderful promise. *"Certainly I will be with you, and this shall be a sign to you that I have sent you: When you have brought the people out of Egypt, you shall serve God in this mountain"* (Ex. 3:12). It is interesting to note He did not say "if'" but "when!" God's plans foretold will always come to pass because His word cannot fail. The first thing God does is to give Moses the **Assurance of His Presence**. *"I will be with you."* This is an awesome promise to go forward with!

God has given strong comfort to many who were facing momentous tasks before them! Think of Jacob running away from home. He took a stone, and laid his head upon it for a night's sleep (Gen. 28:11). That night God revealed Himself in a dream as Jacob saw a ladder, the top of it reaching to heaven. Angels were ascending and descending and the Lord was standing above it. In his dream, the Lord gave a great promise to Jacob. *"Behold, I am with you and will keep you wherever you go, and will bring you back to this land; for I will not leave you until I have done what I have spoken to you"* (Gen. 28:15). When Jacob woke up, he said *"Surely the Lord is in this place, and I did not know it. And he was afraid and said, 'How awesome is this place! This is none other than the house of God, and this is the gate of heaven'"* (Gen. 28:16 NKJV). Consider Joshua, after Moses was dead. He took over the leadership of the people to go over and possess the land. God spoke to him with reassuring words, *"As I was with Moses so shall I be with you"* (Josh. 1:5). Joshua had been in training in the wilderness with Moses and now he was given the responsibility of leadership. He moved forward, knowing the Lord would be with him all the way through. The words of David in Psalm 139:7-10 are strong words of promise:

> *"Whither shall I go from Thy spirit? Or whither shall I flee from Thy presence? If I ascend into heaven, Thou art there: if I make my bed in hell, behold, Thou art there. If I take the wings of the morning, and dwell in the uttermost parts of the sea; even there shall Thy hand lead me, and Thy right hand shall hold me up."*

Once more consider the encouraging words of the Lord to His redeemed people. *"When you pass through the waters I will be with you; and through the rivers they shall not over flow you. When you walk through the fire, you shall not be burned, nor shall the flame scorch you"* (Isa. 43:2 NKJV). What about us today? The words of the writer to the Hebrews are still as treasured as ever, *"I will never leave thee nor forsake thee ... The Lord is my helper; I will not fear what man can do to me"* (Heb. 13:5-6). We can press forward knowing the promise of His abiding presence with us.

God brought to Moses the **Revelation of His Person.** Moses continued to resist. He raised his concern as to whether he would be accepted by his brethren back in Egypt. *"When I say to them The God of our Fathers hath sent me to you they will ask, What is His name? What shall I say unto them?"* (Ex. 3:13). Did Moses think the people were so removed from who God was that they would not know Him? Maybe there was a deep searching in his own soul to learn who God really was. Either way God said to Moses, *"I AM WHO I AM hath sent you. The Lord God of your fathers, the God of Abraham, the God of Isaac, and the God of Jacob have sent me to you. This is My Name forever, and this is my memorial to all generations"* (NKJV). We are here introduced to the One who is eternal and who yet remains the same. He is unchangeable as to His character and unchanging as to his divine program. With such a God by his side, how could Moses fail to do what was asked of him?

Moses is brought to the **Unfolding of His Purpose**. You would have thought that Moses would have been excited by what God was going to do. God says,

> *"I will bring you up out of the affliction of Egypt to the land of the Canaanites and the Hittites and the Amorites and the Perizzites and the Hivites and the Jebusites to a land flowing with milk and honey. So will I stretch out my hand and strike Egypt with all my wonders, which I will do in the midst; and after that he will let you go. And I will give this people favor in the sight of the Egyptians; and it shall be, when you go, that you shall not go empty handed. But every woman shall ask of her neighbour, namely, of her who dwells near her house, articles of silver, articles of gold, and clothing, and you shall put them on your sons and on your daughters. So shall you plunder the Egyptians"* (Ex. 3:17-22).

How could Moses resist such an assurance of what God was going to do through him? But Moses had another objection, excusing him from complete obedience to the Word of God. What if the people would not believe that God was sending him? So again God demonstrated His power by showing to Moses what He could do with a serpent, and a leprous hand, and water taken from the river. Moses is now left with only one other line of resistance, *"O my Lord, I am not an eloquent, neither before or since Thou has spoken to Thy servant, but I am slow of speech and slow of tongue"* (4:10). God's patience was beginning to run out as He rebuked Moses, *"Who made man's mouth? Or who makes the mute, the deaf, the seeing, and the blind? Have not I the Lord?"* (4:11).

It seems Moses put up one last line of defense and asked, *"O my Lord send I pray Thee by the hand of him whom Thou wilt send"* (4:13). At that very moment Aaron the brother of Moses came and the Lord said Aaron would go with him and be his spokesman. All the words that Aaron and Moses would speak would come from God Himself. Eventually, the servant is ready to do His Masters' will.

5

AN UNFORGETABLE NIGHT

We now come to one of the most important chapters in the Bible. Exodus 12 reveals the wonderful deliverance God brought to His people Israel. He did it in a unique and powerful way. *"This month shall be the beginning of months to you"* (12:2). What the people needed more than anything was a completely new start, which would ultimately lead them to a new way of life and a new destiny. Nicodemus had reached this same point when the Lord said to him, *"Ye must be born again"* (John 3:3). The old nature with its way of life, could not be changed or made better. What Nicodemus needed was a completely new life. Only in our Lord Jesus Christ can this new life be found. How could these people, loaded down with heavy burdens, make a fresh new start? All their human efforts were ineffective. Now they have no choice but to leave the answer with the Lord. Did He not promise a way of deliverance from their bondage? When we set this Old Testament picture aside and consider our great deliverer it is thrilling to learn that He was the promised one. Romans 1:1-4 says, *"Which He had promised afore time by His prophets in the Holy Scriptures, concerning His Son Jesus Christ our Lord, which was made of the seed of David according to the flesh; and declared to be the Son of God with power, according to the spirit of holiness, by the resurrection of the dead."* It would be a good exercise to consider some of the Scriptures which relate to this glorious theme.

God gives His command for them to take a **lamb**. He is

introducing us again to that beautiful picture first recorded in Genesis 4:4. The only way a guilty sinner can have a relationship with the living God is through the blood of a slain lamb. Abel's lamb was the basis of his acceptance with God. Here in this chapter we look at another aspect of the necessity for a lamb to be provided. Let's consider the lamb and what it would provide for those people. Of course, in looking at the picture we must keep in mind the Person the picture speaks about.

The Sufficient Lamb (v. 4)

You will notice it says, *"if the household be too little for the lamb,"* they were to share it with their neighbour next to them. This lamb was able to meet the need of every member of the household. When John the Baptist brought the Lord Jesus to the attention of the nation of Israel he said, *"Behold the Lamb of God which taketh away the sin of the world"* (John 1:29). These amazing words remind us that there is not one person in the world who cannot come into blessing through the Lamb of God. The only reason that every one will not be blessed is that some have chosen to reject Him in their hearts. They will face the consequences when they meet the judgment of the Lamb (Rev. 20:11-15). For anyone who is still rejecting the Lord Jesus as the Lamb of God there is still good news. The Lord Jesus died for all sin on the cross. Through the shedding of His blood He is able to cleanse each stain no matter how dark. *"For without the shedding of blood there can be no remission of sins."*

> There was One who was willing to die in my stead,
> That a soul so unworthy might live;
> And the path to the cross He was willing to tread,
> All the sins of my life to forgive.
> They are nailed to the cross, they are nailed to the cross,
> O how much He was willing to bear!
> With what anguish and loss Jesus went to the cross!
> But He carried my sins with Him there.
>
> —Mrs. Frank A. Breck

The Selection of the Lamb (v. 5)

There were certain requirements for the Lamb to be suitable to satisfy the heart of God. The lamb had to be without blemish—without a mark or a flaw. This is a picture of the only One who was *"without blemish and without spot"* (1 Pet. 1:19). The Lord Jesus alone was without sin. Peter said, *"He did no sin neither was guile found in his mouth"* (1 Pet. 2:22). Paul said, *"He knew no sin"* (2 Cor. 5:21). John said, *"In Him is no sin"* (1 Jn. 3:5). The person who would qualify to take the sinner's place had to be one who was absolutely sinless. He did not come from Adam's polluted ancestry, but He was the Lord from heaven. His lovely person shone with His moral glories. The lamb had to be a male of the first year signifying a young, tender lamb. The Lord Jesus died at an early age; He was taken in the prime of His life. The events that led to His crucifixion were not planned by men but He was *"delivered by the determinate council and foreknowledge of God, taken, and by wicked hands was crucified and slain"* (Acts 2:23).

> Guilty, vile and helpless we;
> Spotless Lamb of God was He;
> "Full atonement" can it be?
> Hallelujah! what a Saviour!
> —P. B. Bliss

The acceptable lamb could be taken from the sheep or goats. In this it was identified as one of the flock it was taken from. This brings us to the wonderful fact that *"great is the mystery of godliness: God was manifest in the flesh"* (1 Tim. 3:16). What a tremendous moment in history when this promise of Isaiah was fulfilled: *"Behold the virgin shall be with child, and bear a son, and they shall call His name Immanuel, which is translated God with us"* (Matt. 1:23). The writer to the Hebrews presents some very interesting facts about this one who was born.

> *"Inasmuch then as the children have partaken of flesh and blood, He Himself likewise shared in the same, that through death He might destroy him who had the power of death, that is, the devil, and release those who through*

> *fear of death were all their lifetime subject to bondage"* (Heb. 2:14-15 NKJV).

The writer continues: *"Therefore, in all things He had to be made like His brethren, that He might be a merciful and faithful High Priest in things pertaining to God, to make propitiation for the sins of the people"* (v. 17). John says, *"The Word became flesh and dwelt among us, and we beheld His glory, the glory as of the only begotten of the Father, full of grace and truth"* (John 1:14). Many more references can be given to this truth—that in order for God to deal with our sins He had to take on our likeness (though without sin) and in His body take the punishment for our sin.

> My sin—oh, the bliss of this glorious thought—
> My sin—not in part, but the whole,
> Is nailed to the cross and I bear it no more,
> Praise the Lord, praise the Lord, O my soul!
> —H. G. Spafford

The Sacrifice of the Lamb (v. 6)

We should never tire of looking at the moral glories of our beloved Lord. Yet, these glories could not accomplish our salvation. This lamb had to be taken and killed that evening before the whole assembly of the congregation. This speaks of a corporate responsibility. When John saw the Lord Jesus, he said, *"Behold the Lamb of God who takes away the sin of the world"* (John 1:29). He viewed the sacrifice of the Son of God as being given for the whole of the human race. In writing his first epistle, John reveals to us the extent of this supreme sacrifice by saying, *"He is the propitiation for our sins: and not for ours only, but also for the sins of the whole world"* (2:2). While it is true that He died for all, everyone will not come into the blessings that His sacrifice has made available. The lamb selected from the flock was slain and its blood was shed. This brings us to that momentous time in history when cruel hands took the Lord Jesus and crucified Him. It is here we see the sinless Saviour die for guilty sinners.

Stop for a minute to think about these things. What infinite cost to God to allow His Son to die for you. The words of Isaiah 53:6 say, *"All we like sheep have gone astray; we have turned everyone to his own way; and the Lord hath laid on him the iniquity of us all."* Paul says, *"He who did not spare His own Son, but delivered Him up for us all, how shall He not with Him also freely give us all things"* (Rom. 8:32). There are many Scriptures which relate to this great theme and it would be good for our younger readers to take their concordance and look them up.

O wondrous hour when Jesus, Thou,
Co equal with the Eternal God,
Beneath our sins didst deign to bow,
And in our stead did bear the rod.
—Edward Denny

The Shelter of the Lamb

Here is another interesting aspect of the lamb that was slain. *"Now the blood shall be a sign for you on the houses where you are. And when I see the blood, I will pass over you; and the plague shall not be on you to destroy you when I strike the land of Egypt"* (v. 13). The word for "passover" means a covering over for protection. In other words, when the destroying angel came through the land that night, the firstborn in the house would be safe. But in any house where the blood was not applied, the firstborn would be dead. You see, the blood on the doorposts of their house meant salvation and rejoicing. But, where the blood was not applied, this meant judgment and sorrow. Turning again to the scene at Calvary we see One hanging there for you and for me. The precious blood that flowed from the Saviour was given so that we might have protection from coming judgment. As we look by faith and accept what He accomplished for our sins we shall be saved from wrath to come. Paul, writing his first epistle to the Thessalonians, in 1:9-10 says, *"How they turned to God from idols to serve the living and true God, and to wait for his son from Heaven, whom He raised from the dead, even Jesus who delivers us from the wrath to come."* Isn't this the best news? The administration of God's judgment will never fall on me.

The Sustenance of the Lamb (v. 8-11)

Not only was the lamb to be taken, its blood shed, and applied to the doorposts, but also that night it was roasted with fire. Before they commenced their journey, they fed on the roast lamb to sustain them on the way. We too, having been redeemed by the blood of the Lamb, continually feed upon the wondrous truths of our blessed Saviour. When did you last turn the pages of your Bible and meditate upon the Lamb of God? Do it today, and you will be encouraged in your walk with the Lord!

> O Lamb of God, still keep me
> Near to Thy wounded side;
> 'Tis only there in safety
> And peace I can abide.
> With foes and snares around me!
> And lusts and fears within!
> The grace that sought and found me,
> Alone can keep me clean.
>
> —Jas. G. Deck

Significance of the Lamb

Here we come to a very important aspect of the sacrifice that had been made. That night in which this great deliverance was experienced was never to be forgotten. In verse 24 of our chapter it says, *"And you shall observe this thing as an ordinance for you and your sons forever."* Each year the Passover was kept so that they would not forget they had been bondmen in Egypt. Notice this parallel that the Lord Jesus, before He went to the cross, instituted a memorial feast. He did this when He gathered His disciples in the upper room. Hear His tender words as He took the bread into his hands, gave thanks and said, *"This is My body which is given for you; do this in remembrance of Me. Likewise He also took the cup after supper and said, This cup is the new covenant in My blood, which is shed for you"* (Luke 22:19-20). Is it possible you may be ignoring His simple request to remember Him? The sweetest moments on earth are experienced when gathered with His people to remember Him. Paul, in 1 Corinthians 11:23-26 says,

> *"I have received from the Lord that which I also delivered to you: that the Lord Jesus on the same night in which He was betrayed took bread; and when He had given thanks, He broke it and said, Take, eat; this is My body which is broken for you; do this in remembrance of Me. In the same manner He also took the cup after supper, saying, This cup is the new covenant in My blood. This do, as often as you drink it, in remembrance of Me. For as often as you eat this bread and drink this cup, you proclaim the Lord's death till He comes."*

What a prospect!

Thy body broken for my sake,
My bread from heaven shall be;
Thy testamental cup I take,
And thus remember Thee.

When to the cross I turn my eyes,
And rest on Calvary,
O Lamb of God my sacrifice!
I must remember Thee:

And when, O Lord, Thou com'st again,
And I Thy glory see,
Forever as the Lamb once slain,
I will remember Thee.
—James Montgomery

6

READY FOR THE JOURNEY

One cannot begin to estimate the joy in the hearts of this enslaved people. Never would they forget the experience of that eventful night. What an amazing transformation took place, as they were ready to march out of Egypt forever. Before the journey begins, however, let's consider the tragic consequences to the Egyptian people. Their cruel leader had underestimated the greatness of the God of Israel. Even though he had seen God's tremendous power displayed, he had hardened his heart, and resisted every move God made towards him. Now the sad reality of defeat sank in and he was ready to let the Hebrew people go. *"He called for Moses and Aaron by night, and said, Rise, go out from among my people, both you and the children of Israel. And go, serve the Lord as you have said. Also take your flocks and your herds, as you have said, and be gone; and bless me also"* (12:31-32). As we continue to look at the picture, we see the tragic consequences to those who refuse to accept God's appointed way. The destroying angel brought death to the firstborn son. *"And it came to pass at midnight that the Lord struck all the firstborn in the land of Egypt, from the firstborn of Pharaoh who sat on his throne to the firstborn of the captive who was in the dungeon, and all the firstborn of livestock* (v. 29). Death and judgment reached every corner of the land. But the enslaved people were set free. They were ready to go.

Moses had given some prior instructions to prepare the children of Israel for the journey that lay ahead. In 12:11 he had told them about eating the roast lamb. However, there were certain things which had to be done before they could eat the lamb. They had to eat it with their loins girded. The girded loins spoke of standing strong, ready to march forward. As believers in Christ, we have to put on the whole armour of God, so that we may withstand the onslaught of enemy attack. In Ephesians 6 there is listed for us the complete armour by which we are protected. One part of that armour is to *"have your loins girt about with truth."* Peter, in his epistle says, *"Therefore gird up the loins of your mind, be sober, and rest your hope fully on the grace that is to be brought unto you at the revelation of Jesus Christ"* (1 Pet. 1:13). In principle, we see how important the truth of God is for all our lives. The first evidence that a person has new life in Christ is their deep desire to learn the truths of Scripture. When a baby is born, it has an instinctive craving for milk. *"As new born babes, desire the pure milk of the word, that you may grow thereby"* (1 Pet. 2:2). I encourage each reader to get into a sincere study of the Word of God! You need to be strong and courageous to live for the Lord Jesus in today's society. There is no substitute for reading, studying, and meditating upon the Word. This will enable you to be a *"workman that needeth not to be ashamed, rightly dividing the word of truth"* (2 Tim. 2:15). Concentrate your minds on what Paul wrote in Philippians 4:8:

> *Whatsoever things are true, whatsoever things are honest, whatsoever things are just, whatsoever things are pure, whatsoever things are lovely, whatsoever things are of good report; if there be any virtue, and if there be any praise, think on these things. Those things, which you have both learned, and received, and heard, and seen in me, do: and the God of peace shall be with you.*

David says, *"I hate vain thoughts: but thy law do I love* (Ps. 119:113). In the same Psalm he says, *"make me to understand the way of thy precepts: so shall I talk of thy wondrous works* (v. 27). When you learn the truth you will want to share it with others so that they too will be blessed. Are your loins girded with the Truth of God?

Moses commanded them to eat the Passover *"with their shoes on their feet"*! Coming back to the armour in Ephesians 6:15 we notice the exhortation for your feet to be shod *"with the preparation of the gospel of peace"*. Our feet play a very important role in the function of our bodies. The whole weight of the body rests upon the feet. In other words, the feet are the foundation upon which the body stands and the means by which the body moves. When we apply this fact to the body of Christ, the church, we see the tremendous responsibility the church has for the preaching of the gospel. Unfortunately, many assemblies today are setting aside the public preaching of the gospel of the grace of God. This means that the local assembly is not functioning in the way that God intended it to. The prophet in Isaiah 52:7 says, *"How beautiful upon the mountains are the feet of him who bring good news, who proclaims peace; who brings glad tidings of good things, who proclaims salvation; who says to Zion, Thy God reigneth."* This is a beautiful prophetic statement regarding our Lord Jesus Christ! When the Lord read, in the synagogue, the words from the same prophet He said, *"The Spirit of the Lord is upon Me, because He has anointed Me to preach the gospel to the poor; He has sent Me to heal the brokenhearted, to proclaim liberty to the captives, and recovery of sight to the blind, to set at liberty those who are oppressed, to proclaim the acceptable year of the Lord"* (Luke 4:18). The writer to the Hebrews describes this salvation as that *"which at the first began to be spoken by the Lord, and was confirmed to us by those who heard Him"* (2:3). We read so often in the Gospels that Jesus went about the cities and villages preaching the Gospel. What an example He has left for us to follow! After His resurrection, He commissioned His disciples to go into the world and preach the Gospel. Paul, in Romans 10:14-15, brings this commissioning right up to date as he challenges the believers by saying,

> *"How then shall they call on him in whom they have not believed? And how shall they believe in Him of whom they have not heard? And how shall they hear without a preacher? And how shall they preach, unless they are sent? As it is written, How beautiful are the feet of those who preach the gospel of peace, who bring glad tidings of good things!*

Notice, that what began with the Lord has now been passed on to the disciples to fulfill.

However, not everyone has believed the gospel. For Isaiah said, *"Lord, who has believed our report? So then, faith comes by hearing, and hearing by the word of God."* Are you, as a believer, in a position of readiness? *"But sanctify the Lord God in your hearts: and be ready always to give an answer to every one that asks you, a reason of the hope that is within you with meekness and fear"* (1 Pet. 3:15). Is your assembly fulfilling its responsibility like the Thessalonians who *"sounded out the Word of the Lord"* (1 Thess. 1:8), or like the Philippians who were *"holding forth the word of life"* (Phil. 2:16)? Are you marching on to the land of promise by having "your feet shod?"

Lastly, they were to *"have their staff in their hand."* The staff is used in three different ways. Jacob, according to Hebrews 11:21, *"when he was dying, blessed both the sons of Joseph; and worshipped leaning upon the top of his staff."* This is a beautiful picture of an old man having a place to lean while he worshipped his God. Depth of worship in the local assembly will only come when room has been given in each individual heart for God's Word. True worship ascends when the soul, occupied with the Scriptures, is given a deeper appreciation of the Lord Jesus Christ and His accomplishments at Calvary. Secondly, this word "staff" is the same word used for the staves in the tabernacle. They were used by the priests for carrying the vessels of the sanctuary through the wilderness. Here another lesson is presented when in our priestly service we bear the vessels that speak of our Lord. Are you fulfilling your responsibilities here in this scene of His rejection? Thirdly, David did not fear the *"valley of the shadow of death"* (Ps. 23) because the rod and staff were a comfort to him. The shepherd's staff is another aspect of the Word of God as it ministers in times of deep need. Having complied with divine instructions the people were ready to march forward. The urgency of the moment inspired immediate obedience.

7

THE JOURNEY BEGINS

Many more lessons can be learned from the 12th chapter of Exodus. We could examine the shelter and protection provided by the blood or the preservation of the memorial Passover. This feast was set up to be observed every year. Participation in this feast was a reminder to them *"that they were bondmen in Egypt."* The Lord also, on the night in which he was betrayed, instituted a feast for us to remember Him. The disciples were to observe the Lord's supper on the first day of the week with the simple emblems of bread and wine (Acts 20:7). We too can remember the Lamb of God, whose life was given for us in this way. His precious blood shed at Calvary provided our salvation and deliverance from sin. Never let us forget *"the pit from which we have been dug and the rock from which we have been hewn* (Isa. 51:1).

The meaning of all these events surrounding the passover had to be taught to the children of the Israelites. What responsibilities are laid upon parents, Sunday School teachers, youth and Bible class leaders to teach the children why we practice the things we do. At the end of the chapter we see the Israelites' complete obedience to all that was communicated to them. The prelude to all blessing is implicit obedience to all that is commanded. Time and time again this principle is seen in God's dealings with those who are His own. The first marks of their love and appreciation are noted in their willingness to do all He asked of them. Is there the same response in your heart? Are you struggling with full and total surrender? Maybe, deep down, you know what His Word is telling you to do. However, there is a BUT! Does He have the whole of your heart or just a part? I feel the challenge as I write. There is always the danger that our relationship with Him can grow cold. But one of the best ways to keep in close touch with the Saviour is to fulfill His request, *"This do in remembrance of me"* (1 Cor. 11:24).

The mighty blow given to Pharaoh released his grip upon the Israelites. Now he was willing to let them go and to take their flocks and herds with them. This great army moved forward on a three day journey to the Red Sea and into the wilderness. But even en route to the wilderness some interesting things happened. They came to a city called Ramesis. This city had been built by the Israelites as a treasure city for Pharaoh (Ex. 1:11). Now it became a place where God's people were brought from poverty into riches. The Egyptians gave them jewels of silver and gold and raiment (v. 36).

This principle reminds us that we too have come from spiritual bankruptcy into immense wealth. Paul prays for the Ephesian Christians desiring, *"that the eyes of your understanding being enlightened; that you may know what is the hope of His calling, what are the riches of the glory of His inheritance in the saints"* (Eph. 1:18). Speaking to them in 2:7 he says, *"that in the ages to come He might show the exceeding riches of His grace in His kindness toward us through Christ Jesus."* When he writes to the church at Philippi in appreciation for the gift received from them he says, *"My God shall supply all your need according to His riches in glory by Christ Jesus"* (Phil. 4:19). The riches we have in Christ are not material, but spiritual; not earthly, but heavenly; not temporal, but eternal. Now with all this wealth given to you, are you entering into a personal enjoyment of it?

Some time ago I read of an old man who lived in a little wooden shack just outside the city of London, England. He often sat by an old oil stove trying to keep himself warm. One day he was found dead of malnutrition, his body frost bitten from the cold. Later, the authorities traced the background of this down and out tramp. To their surprise they found he was a multi millionaire. Unfortunately, he had chosen to abandon his family and friends for that sad lifestyle. He could have lived and dined at the city's best hotels but he chose otherwise. He was a wealthy man but he elected to live like a pauper. We have to admit that we sometimes live a little bit like that. Having all this wealth in our great Redeemer, we often do not enter into the personal enjoyment of it! These treasures are ours as believers in Christ. Go in and possess them to the full!

The Israelites continued on the journey and came to a place called Succoth. It is here that a mixed multitude joined them along the way. We are not told who these people were but they had not come under the blood of the lamb. As they journeyed through the wilderness this group became a thorn in the flesh to the people of God. They were murmurers, complainers, and indulged their lustful desires. They caused Israel to sin. How many have joined the assembly of the Lord's people but have not been truly saved? There is no evidence in their lives to the reality of what they profess with their lips. Judas Iscariot was a fitting example, for he was numbered with the disciples (Acts 1:17). However, the time came when he took up his place with the enemies of our Saviour. What a price he paid to get thirty pieces of silver! He said *"I have betrayed the innocent blood"* (Matt. 27:4). Paul warns the elders at Ephesus, *"After my departing grievous wolves will come in not sparing the flock"* (Acts 20:29). Beware of counterfeit religion! Be on your guard to discern the false from the true!

It is at Succoth where the firstborn had to be sanctified. In other words, the firstborn became the possession of the Lord: *"both of man and beast; it is Mine"* (Ex. 13:2). This illustrates another important principle, that we are not only **saved** but also **sanctified.** This means we are set apart to God and for God. We are, according to Hebrews 12:23, *"the church of the firstborn."* The church has been purchased by precious blood and is sanctified through redeeming grace. It is God's building and His cultivated field (1 Cor. 3:9).

As they journeyed to the Promised Land, they carried

with them the bones of Joseph. The contents of this coffin-box remind them of the death of their saviour, Joseph, but it would also give assurance of His promise that they would one day possess the land. When the emblems of bread and wine are set before us on the table, we are reminded of our Saviour's death, and of the promise of His coming again. This blessed hope is kept alive every time we remember Him.

So leaving Succoth behind the people moved forward under divine direction and camped at Etham on the edge of the wilderness. It is here that we read of the pillar of cloud which was over them by day and the pillar of fire by night. The symbols of His divine presence would go with them all the way through the wilderness. Even in times when they failed Him and murmured, His presence was always with them. We also have that wonderful assurance, for the Lord said, *"I will never leave you nor forsake you"* (Heb. 13:5).

8

A CHANGE OF HEART

From Etham the people moved to Pihahiroth where they pitched their tents right at the edge of the Red Sea. Although things had gone quite smoothly so far for the Israelites, back in Egypt, Pharaoh's heart was beginning to change. After three days, he realized all the work done by his Hebrew servants had come to an end. He listened to the complaints of his own Egyptian people who now had to do things for themselves. All the slaves had gone! As far as the Egyptians were concerned Pharaoh had made a big mistake by letting the Israelites go. Pharoah found out that the children of Israel were nearing the Red Sea and where they would be closed in. This cruel king quickly forgot the power of the God who had delivered them from his grasp. Pharaoh still thought of himself as the all-powerful one. Remember, however, that nothing is beyond the control of the God of Abraham, Isaac and Jacob. The Lord spoke to Moses and told him what Pharaoh was planning to do. In the past He had spoken many times to Pharaoh revealing His Person, by displaying His great power. Now, through Pharaoh, He was ready to reveal the same fact to the Egyptians. He said, *"I will harden Pharaoh's heart, so that he will pursue them; and I will gain honor over Pharaoh and over all his army, that the Egyptians may know that I am the Lord"* (Ex. 14:4). The time had come for God to make Himself fully known to the Egyptians.

Pharaoh wasted no time getting his mighty army ready for the pursuit. He took six hundred of his best military captains with their chariots and horses for the battle. Before long they arrived near the Israelites' encampment and quickly prepared for attack. You can imagine the panic on the faces of the Israelites as they saw their old enemy approaching. It is at this point that God's redeemed people sowed their first seeds of murmuring and complaining. They said to Moses, *"Because there were no graves in Egypt, have you taken us away to die in the wilderness? Why have you dealt with us, to bring us up out of Egypt?"* (v. 11). They came to the conclusion, *"it would have been better for us to serve the Egyptians than that we should die in the wilderness"* (v. 12). The one who had led them out in great triumph is now the brunt of accusation and complaint.

Not infrequently do true leaders of God's people come under evil attack when things start to go wrong. God's people today in the assembly are no different than these Israelites. God has given a plurality of elders the responsibility to oversee, feed, lead, guide and guard the local church. We must love, respect, honour and obey these elders. It is a serious thing to despise God-given authority. But notice the confident way Moses handled the situation. He showed the true mark of a spiritual leader as he calmed the fears of the people saying, *"Do not be afraid. Stand still, and see the salvation of the Lord, which He will accomplish for you today. For the Egyptians whom you see today, you shall see again no more forever. The Lord will fight for you, and you shall hold your peace"* (Ex. 14:13-14). Moses did not see the power of the enemy as a threat because his confidence was in the Lord his God! Paul says, in Romans 8:31, *"If God be for us who can be against us?"* Maybe today, you are coming under constant attack from the Evil One. Don't doubt or be afraid for *"greater is He that is in you than he that is in the world"* (1 Jn. 4:4).

Although Moses had directed the people to stand still, this was not the divine intention for them. In fact God gave Moses a stern rebuke, *"Why do you cry to Me? Tell the children of Israel to go forward"* (Ex. 14:15). Often we fail when we bring our petitions to the Lord and He has already given us the answer through His Word! Far too frequently we really want our own way instead of being obedient to what He has revealed. There was to be no stopping or standing still for this people—at least not yet. They were on a journey to a promised land and the only way was forward. Where are you right now in your spiritual life? Going backward, standing still, or going forward? It is good to take inventory and to examine your condition and position on the spiritual pathway. To stand still would have meant certain defeat! To go forward, even though the path was unknown, meant victory!

God gave Moses another command, *"Lift up your rod, and stretch out your hand over the sea and divide it. And the children of Israel will go on dry ground through the midst of the sea"* (14:16). What excitement must have gripped the heart of Moses as he waited to see another exhibition of God's great and mighty power. God not only revealed what He was going to do for Israel, but He also told him what would be the fate of the Egyptians: *"I indeed will harden the hearts of the Egyptians, and they shall follow them. So I will gain honour over Pharaoh, his chariots, and his horsemen"* (14:17). God often gives a preview as to what He will accomplish so that we may stand in awe of Him, who knows the end from the beginning. There is nothing which overtakes Him by chance. He is in complete control all the time.

This chapter records one of the most dramatic events in the Bible. Having been told by God what was about to happen, they settled in for the night before the crossing. We come now to another important truth, which is Israel's divine protection. *"And the Angel of God who went before the camp of Israel, moved and went behind them; and the pillar of cloud went from before them and stood behind them. So it came between the camp of the Egyptians and the camp of Israel. Thus it was a cloud and darkness to the one, and it gave light by night to the other, so that the one did not come near the other all that night"* (14:19-20). Here is presented the great truth of separation. There are many times this fact is brought to us when light is contrasted with darkness. They can't exist together simultaneously, for when the light comes in, darkness is dispelled. And today, when so many who call themselves Christians are associating with the things that belong in the realm of darkness, spiritual progress is seriuosly hampered. We are reminded today of our unique position in Christ: *"You are all sons of light and sons of the day. We are not of the night or darkness"* (1 Thess. 5:5). Not only was the night filled with light, but they also had angelic protection guaranteeing their complete safety. Notice that Israel as a nation has always enjoyed angelic protection. This will be true for them in the future as well (Dan. 12:1). Another interesting feature was that the cloud that led them moved behind them. The cloud, being a symbol of the Presence of God, meant that all of heaven was hedged around them. No matter how powerful their enemy was, Israel was secure and safe.

Moses took his rod and stretched it out over the sea. All that night, God caused a strong east wind to divide the waters. Although the dividing of the waters was by supernatural power, God uses the elements of nature to accomplish His purpose. He does this often in the Word of God. Again this would be a good exercise for the young Christian to search out other occasions to illustrate this fact. He uses the things that are present and adds His divine touch to them. Because Moses did what God asked him to do, God was able to do the rest. Once again, the truth is clear: obedience is the prelude to blessing. Are you today obeying His Word or rebelling against it? This weak and failing people were so amazed as they all crossed over the Red Sea on dry ground. The Egyptians, trying to take advantage of the highway provided, forgot about the God who had opened up this way. As Moses lifted up his rod a second time, God allowed the waters to come crashing down. All the Egyptians were drowned.

Before we leave this amazing scene let us consider its spiritual significance. In 1 Corinthians chapter 10, Paul looks at this picture and says, *"Moreover brethren, I do not want you to be unaware that all our fathers were under the cloud, all passed through the sea, all were baptized unto Moses in the cloud and in the sea"* (vv. 1-2). The people had left Egypt behind forever. They were moving onward with a new Commander-in-Chief. The power and authority of Pharaoh was broken and they were under new leadership. Paul, in Romans chapter 6 (read the chapter), brings the wonderful truth that we too are under a new leadership. For the believer, the power of sin and Satan has been conquered! The Lord Jesus Christ is now the One we worship and serve. If this is true of you, have you obeyed His Word by being baptized and by giving testimony to your personal faith in Him as Saviour and Lord? Paul was writing to those who had already been baptized, challenging them as to its daily effect in their lives. The teaching for us is clear: for we have a people who are **saved**, **sanctified**, and **separated**.

9

A SONG TO SING

Imagine the tremendous feeling of freedom the children of Israel experienced after they had crossed the Red Sea! To their amazement and astonishment, all their enemies were drowned in the sea. What jubilation and excitement arose within the camp of Israel! The terrifying night was over and the morning was filled with singing. This is the first time we read of singing in the Bible. The sound of music filled the air and it would have been a pleasure to have listened to it. In fact, if we had been there, we would have joined in the melody and harmony of that song. Many words have been written and sung since then, but none so sweet as the song of Redemption.

This is not only the first song in the Bible but its lyrics are to be found again in Revelation 15:3 where it will be sung once more: *"They sing the song of Moses, the servant of God, and the song of the Lamb, saying: Great and marvellous are Thy works, Lord God Almighty: Just and true are Thy ways, Thou King of saints."* When the seven last plagues have been executed upon the earth by the wrath of God, a great victory will have been accomplished. The beast with his image and mark are defeated, and once again redemption's song is sung! It is worthy of note that the true Lamb, our Lord Jesus Christ, is the mighty Conqueror!

Let us examine carefully the contents of the song that ascended from their hearts. The theme and words expressed here are well worth our special consideration. Many songs have plenty of repetition accompanied by loud music but they lack spiritual depth. Here the words and music were presented to God out of deep, personal experience and exercise. The main theme of this first song was the person of the LORD God of Israel. The wonder of who He is and the power of His accomplishments gave rise to adoration and worship! But we have been brought into greater blessings than Israel ever experienced. Do you make Him the theme of your praise? Is He alone the object of your worship? Or have you lost the joy of your salvation, having no song in your heart? It is time to 'turn your eyes upon Jesus', realizing once again the reality of Him in your soul. How great He is! No matter what your circumstances are today, He still loves you with His everlasting love. He wants you to bow at His feet and to know the restoration and forgiveness of His marvelous grace. Then you can sing once more the song of the redeemed.

You can never lose your salvation, but you can lose its joy. Consider David's soul search in Psalm 51:8: *"Make me hear joy and gladness; that the bones you have broken may rejoice"* (v. 12), *"Restore to me the joy of Your salvation; and uphold me by your generous Spirit."* Once our joy and song are restored, there are great benefits that accompany them. *"Then I will teach transgressors Your ways, and sinners shall be converted to You"* (v. 13). Remember when God's people were down in Babylon. They said, *"We hanged our harps upon the willows."* They *"wept when they remembered Zion."* Those who required of them a song of Zion were told *"How can we sing the Lord's song in a strange land"* (Ps. 137:4). Years in captivity had drowned the Lord's songs in their tears. What about you? Paul exhorts us in Ephesians 5:19, *"Speaking to yourselves in psalms and hymns and spiritual songs, singing and making melody in your heart to the Lord."* Colossians 3:16 says, *"Let the Word of Christ dwell in you richly in all wisdom; teaching and admonishing one another in psalms and hymns and spiritual songs, singing with grace in your hearts to the Lord."*

A Song of Triumph

"The horse and its rider He has thrown into the sea" (v. 1).

At an earlier stage, we looked at the horse as a symbol of

strength and power. All the might of Egypt was displayed in the horses and chariots of Pharaoh. When the people heard their hoofs thundering in hot pursuit to take them back to captivity, they were afraid. They watched with fear as these same horses galloped into the pathway through the sea that God had opened. But at the perfect moment they saw God release the walls of water on either side. With great terror the Egyptians were trapped as they plunged into a watery grave. Not one of them survived the mighty waves that came down upon them. Everyone was drowned, and *"the Lord hath triumphed gloriously."* All the praise went to the One to whom it rightly belonged—the Lord Himself!

This was a Song of Testimony

"He is become my salvation" (v. 2).

Now the wonderful reality of what had taken place gripped their hearts. Even the nations round about heard what great things God had done for His people. At a later date, David wrote in Psalm 126:2-3: *"Then said they among the nations, The Lord hath done great things for them. The Lord hath done great things for us, and we are glad."* You and I have been saved with a greater salvation than Israel ever experienced. It is described in Hebrews 2:3 as *"so great salvation"!* This salvation was provided at such an infinite cost through the blood of God's own Son. He accomplished a great victory on the cross when He defeated the enemy of the human race. Do you have a testimony to tell? Have you experienced His delivering power? It is communicated to us by the gospel. Paul says in Romans 1:16 *"I am not ashamed of the gospel of Christ, for it is the power of God unto salvation to every one who believes."* Faith believes the message of the gospel and brings the sinner into a relationship with God. The blood of Jesus Christ is still the only power that is able to cleanse the soul from sin and to change the life completely. *"Therefore, if any one is in Christ, he is a new creation; old things have passed away; behold, all things have become new"* (2 Cor. 5:17).

A Song of Worship (vv. 3-12)

Each expression rises to give praise to the Lord because

of who He is and what He had accomplished. Notice verse 3: *"The Lord is a man of war: the Lord is His Name."* These word pictures portray this One, who is so high and lofty, in terms they can understand. Paul says it this way, that He *"being in the form of God, did not consider it robbery to be equal with God, but made Himself of no reputation, taking the form of a bond servant, and coming in the likeness of men. And being found in appearance as a man, He humbled Himself and became obedient to the point of death, even the death of the cross"* (Phil. 2:6-8). This is indeed a wonderful truth that God became a man and identified Himself with us so that we, in turn, can have a relationship with God. John so beautifully presents it to us in John 1:14: *"The Word became flesh and dwelt among us, and we beheld His glory, the glory as of the only begotten of the Father, full of grace and truth."* Paul sums it up by saying *"And without controversy great is the mystery of godliness: God was manifest in the flesh"* (1 Tim. 3:16). To accomplish His great victory He had to become a man. So we can exclaim like Thomas, *"my Lord and my God!"*

Here we have Moses record of exactly what the Lord had done, and how He did it! *"Pharaoh's chariots and his army He has cast into the sea"* (v. 4). *"Your right hand, O Lord has dashed the enemy in pieces"* (v. 6). *"You sent forth Your wrath. It consumed them like stubble"* (v. 7). *"With the blast of Your nostrils the waters were gathered together"* (v. 8). *"You blew Your wind and the sea covered them"* (v. 10). *"You stretched out Your right hand; The earth swallowed them"* (v. 12). Never let us forget how He defeated all our enemies! The way He did it was on the cross—a mighty deed was done!

> Lest I forget Gethsemane;
> Lest I forget Thine agony;
> Lest I forget Thy love to me,
> Lead me to Calvary.
> —Jennie Evelyn Hussey

A Song of Truth (vv .13-18)

The real purpose God had called them out of Egypt is revealed in this wonderful song they are singing! *"You in Your mercy have led forth the people whom You have redeemed; You have guided them in Your strength to Your holy habitation."* He could never be in the midst of His people until they were brought to Himself in the wilderness. This is also true of our situation today. God has saved us so we might become His people and that we would gather together to Him. Amid all the religious confusion in Christendom, we may be encouraged to know there are many companies of the Lord's people gathered in His Name throughout the world. He still has that special place afforded Him. However, many churches, like Laodicea, are leaving Him outside the door, knocking for admission (Rev. 3:20).

Another reason God called them out of Egypt is given in verse 17: *"You will bring them in, and plant them in the mountain of Your inheritance, in the place, O Lord, which You have made for Your own dwelling in the sanctuary, O Lord, which Your hands have established."* The word "sanctuary" simply means a clean place. God had designed this as the place where He could take up His residence among His people. He also designed a means whereby they could approach Him. This will be taken up in a later chapter.

A Song of Thanksgiving (vv. 20-21)

Here the women joined in the praise. Miriam led with a timbrel in her hand. Sometimes we underestimate the tremendous role the women play in corporate worship. While their place is to be silent in the church (1 Cor. 14:33-35) and is not a place of leading or teaching, nevertheless there are many ways in which they are encouraged to participate. Here in Exodus the women gather to express their thanksgiving to the God who had brought this great deliverance. We think of some of the important roles the sisters have played in their service for the Lord. Mary had the privilege of communicating the word to the disciples that the Lord was alive. Lydia opened her home for the care of the servants of God. Dorcas made coats and garments to give to the poor and needy. Phoebe was a servant of the church and a helper of many. The woman in 1 Timothy 5:10, before she was widowed, was *"well reported of for good works; if she have brought up children, if she have lodged strangers, if she have washed the saints' feet, if she have relieved the afflicted, if she have diligently followed every good work."* The older women have to teach the younger women (Tit. 2:4) and so the list goes on. There is much for the women to do that is honouring to the Lord. Many men may gladly let them take their responsibilities as well, but God has very clearly defined gender roles. However, in the context of this passage, the women's joy was complete as they worshipped the God who is worthy to be praised. Once again, we need to ask ourselves, are we singing redemption's song?

10

NEW EXPERIENCES IN THE WAY

But now the wonderful song, which had begun in their hearts, had to cease. It was time to press on in the journey which lay before them. We are told in Exodus 15:22 that they went a three days' journey into the wilderness. When they arrived, they found no water for them to drink. This was their first major setback along the way. It didn't take long for the singing to change to sighing. Thus began a pattern throughout their journey—a habit of murmuring and complaining in difficult times. After all they had witnessed of the power of God, yet here they were expressing their outrage at their new leader, Moses. How often the Lord's people complain against the leadership, which God has given to them. God in His wisdom has so designed, in this era of grace, that His people would be governed by a plurality of elders. Do we also centre our complaints on them? Are they the objects of our disrespect? Do we point the finger of blame at them when things don't go the way we think they should? Rather we should draw alongside our elders and give them encouragement, appreciating the enormous responsibility upon their shoulders. Make them the subject of your prayers that the Lord would give them wisdom for the tasks before them.

They were murmuring because the waters they had come to drink were bitter. Just imagine what it must have been like for them. To be thirsty and yet unable to drink, for the bitter water could not satisfy nor quench their thirst. This is clearly a picture of this world of ours, with all its attractions catering to masses who are endlessly trying to find something that will truly satisfy. The prophet Jeremiah summed it up well when he said, *"For my people have committed two evils; they have forsaken Me, the fountain of living waters, and hewn out cisterns, broken cisterns, that can hold no water"* (Jer. 2:13). The woman who came to Sychar's well to draw water soon learned who the fountain of living waters was. If you read her story in John chapter 4, you will discover that the water she was drinking could not take away her thirst. She came to the well for a refill day after day, symbolizing the empty pleasure of this world's polluted stream.

These waters of Marah were bitter! Sin has left so much emptiness, pain and heartache. Many homes have been broken, husbands and wives have separated, children are disturbed, young people are giving themselves over to immoral lifestyles, and the list goes on. The biggest problem in every country in the world is the effects of personal sin. The Bible says, *"For all have sinned and come short of the glory of God"* (Rom. 3:23). Have you faced the fact that you're included in that little word "all"? The good news is that God has provided a remedy through His Son in that He died for your sins.

He not only died, but He also rose again from the dead and is waiting for you to receive Him as your personal Lord and Saviour. The woman at the well became irresistibly drawn to Jesus, for He offered her what she could not obtain anywhere else. Listen to His words: *"If you knew the gift of God, and who it is who says to you, 'Give Me a drink,' you would have asked Him, and He would have given you living water"*. Later He says to her, *"Whoever drinks of this water shall thirst again, but whoever drinks of the water that I shall give him … will become a fountain of living water springing up into everlasting life* (John 4:10-14 NKJV). Have you come to the source of eternal life yet? Maybe you have tried everything there is and yet something still is missing. Here is your answer. It is the Lord Jesus Christ. He is waiting for your response.

It is to Moses' credit that he listened patiently to their

complaints and did not retaliate verbally. The longer Moses put up with this people, the more he displayed his tremendous patience and longsuffering. Not only did he listen to them but he also interceded with God on their behalf. Here is the mark of a true leader! Is there an elder in an assembly today, discouraged by the continual problems that the Lord's people bring to you? Remember the experiences of Moses and learn from them. The godly man resorts to prayer and brings the whole matter before the throne of God. What a difference when we take the matters to the Lord, for He alone has the remedy for the situation. There is nothing that can take Him by surprise! He always provides the solutions and in this situation, He gave Moses instruction what to do. I wonder how many difficult problems in assembly life would disappear if more help was sought in prayer. We try to work things out using our human reasoning instead of asking the Lord for direction through His Word.

Now, *"the Lord showed him a tree. When he cast it into the waters, the waters were made sweet"* (15:25). First, we have the revelation given, and what he saw was a tree. We can today look by faith at another tree, where our Lord was crucified. This horrific, yet wondrous sight was the revelation mankind needed to solve all their problems and doubts. The cross was not only an historical event, but it brought to us all the fullness of the love of God. God's estimation of our sin was seen at Calvary in that, *"He laid on Him the iniquity of us all"* (Isa. 53:6). Christ bore our sins on the cross and no human thought can understand it nor heart comprehend it. In Exodus, the tree was cast into the waters and the bitter waters became sweet. Jesus Christ took the bitterness out of our lives which sin had caused, and He gave us sweetness and joy. When the tree touched the waters a wonderful change occurred. Christ's work on the cross can do so much for you, but you need to apply it to your heart and life. These blessings come the moment you recognize you are that sinner for whom He died, and accept, by faith, the Lord Jesus Christ as your personal Saviour. Throughout this book we remind you of the importance of making this choice. Have you made it yet? If not what is keeping you back? To delay will have serious eternal consequences!

At this beginning stage of the journey, God had given them their first test. Time and again, He brought them through various trials to demonstrate what was really in their hearts. How miserably they failed, yet He gave them the opportunity to listen to His commandments, and to be obedient to them. He promised that all the diseases He put upon the Egyptians would not come upon them, if they would obey His commands. The blessings given to Israel were conditional upon their implicit obedience. For us today, all our blessings are unconditional, in Christ. However, He expects our complete obedience to His Word, not out of rigid compliance to rules, but out of love, willingly and voluntary from our hearts. Our obedience is not to be out of a sense of duty, but out of worship and appreciation for all that He has done for us.

After this trying experience, they travelled *"to Elim where there were twelve wells of water, seventy palm trees: and they camped there by the waters"* (15:27). God was so kind to lead them on to this quiet place of rest and refreshment. He is the true Shepherd of Israel whom David knew by experience. *"He leadeth me beside the still waters. He restoreth my soul"* (Ps. 23:2-3). How true it is in the experiences of a believers life. The Lord always brings a calm after the storm. However, this was just a resting place. Although this was needed, it was not their final destination. They probably could have settled down here for a long time. This was only a foretaste of better things to come. Is it possible we are trying to make our haven of rest here in this condemned world? We need to keep in mind we are just pilgrims passing through! The best comforts we can enjoy here are only temporal, but the blessings that await us are eternal. Let us keep our eyes fixed on the things that really matter.

Before we leave this section, it is important to see that God made full provision for all their need. No matter what state or condition they were in, He would always remain faithful to them. What He promised them, He would bring to pass, and His Word could never, ever fail. When you read the last few verses of chapter fifteen, you can feel the wonderful atmosphere of tranquility and peace. I will leave you there for a moment, that you may stop and consider the even greater spiritual environment God has placed us in! I trust you will today consider all that God has done for you.

When upon life's billows you are tempest tossed,
When you are discouraged, thinking all is lost,
Count your many blessings, name them one by one,
And it will surprise you what the Lord has done.

Are you ever burdened with a load of care?
Does the cross seem heavy you are called to bear?
Count your many blessings, every doubt will fly,
And you will be singing as the days go by.

Count your blessing name them one by one;
Count your blessings, see what God hath done;
Count your blessings, name them one by one;
Cound your many blessings, see what God hath done.
—Johnson Oatman, Jr.

11

BREAD FROM HEAVEN

It would have been a pleasure for the people to stay at Elim. However, the journey was only beginning and God had many more experiences for them to go through. They camped at Elim, there enjoying the peaceful atmosphere when something happened to disturb their rest. The cloud started to move. This was an indication that it was time to take down their tents and move on. To wait behind would have spelled disaster for them.

As we consider the meaning of this, we too should be ready to move on at the Lord's leading. Sometimes we don't like it when our comfort is disturbed. It is apprehension of the unknown way that arouses our concern and anxiety. Yet, it is better to move on with the Lord, than to stay behind without Him. Yes, He will always remain with us, but what will we miss if we do not follow His leading! Let's see what lay in store for the children of Israel.

They journeyed from Elim, passing through the wilderness of Sin, on their way to Sinai. It is here that they once again started to murmur and complain. Their minds went back to Egypt, and in their hunger they remembered the pots of meat and bread to eat. They had already forgotten their heavy burdens and enslaved condition in Egypt. They forgot all about their mighty deliverer. The Red Sea experience now seemed insignificant as they felt God had brought them out into the desert to die. Moses and Aaron now came under a heavy barrage of accusations and misunderstandings. The Israelites thought their leaders had ulterior motives in bringing them into the wilderness—that they might go hungry and die. Just think how much these two servants of God had done for them! Is it possible today that you are a believer who looks only on the temporal things and what benefits you can get out of life now? Are you at this moment questioning the God in whom you have put your trust? Has He brought you through a severe trial? Do you think the trial is God's punishment for something you have done? Consider once again, "What great things He has done for you." His mercies are so great that whatever the trial or pain you are passing through, the outcome is for your good. *"We know that all things work together for good to them who love God, to them who are called according to His purpose"* (Rom. 8:28). Trust Him. He knows the end from the beginning.

God responded to their complaining in His patient way by revealing that He would *"rain bread from Heaven for you"* (Ex. 16:4). No matter what need the people had, God was more than able to meet it. There is no lack in His infinite resources. When the cry ascends, He moves in to supply bountifully. Even in spite of their weak and wayward hearts, He was ready and faithful to provide. God was going to show His wonderful faithfulness to them no matter what their circumstances. This is true to His very character, in that He constantly waits to bless all who seek Him. It is interesting to note that this is the first mention of the glory of the Lord. *"In the morning you shall see the glory of the Lord; for He heareth your murmurings against the Lord: and what are we that you murmur against us"* (Ex. 16:7). This is the glory of the Lord: when they murmured against Him, He poured out bread and not the wrath they deserved.

Let us look closely at some things about this bread they were about to receive. I would like you to notice its source. It came from heaven. There was nothing quite like it on earth! The Lord Jesus reminded his hearers in John 6:47-51:

> *Verily, verily, I say unto you, He that believeth on me hath everlasting life. I am that bread of life. Your fathers did eat manna in the wilderness, and are dead. This is the*

> *true bread which cometh down from heaven, that a man may eat thereof, and not die. I am the living bread which came down from heaven: if any man eat of this bread, he shall live forever: and the bread that I will give is my flesh, which I will give for the life of the world.*

We see therefore, a beautiful picture in the manna of the true and living bread—our Lord Jesus Christ. The fact that He came from heaven tells us of His deity. When there was no answer to meet the need of the human race, God Himself left the heavenly sphere to come down and take our place at Calvary. *"God was in Christ, reconciling the world unto Himself"* (2 Cor. 5:19). This Holy One, who bore our sins on the cross, was none other than God Himself.

When the manna came down for the people, observe its location. After the dew had gone up, the wilderness was covered with this heavenly food. This meant the bread was within reach of every one of the people. Had this fallen upon trees only a limited group would have obtained it. The coming down to the ground speaks of His incarnation. We wonder at His lowly birth!

> *"Behold, a virgin shall be with child, and shall bring forth a son, and they shall call His name Emmanuel, which being interpreted is, God with us"* (Matt. 1:23).

> *"The Word was made flesh, and dwelt among us, and we beheld His glory, the glory as of the only begotten of the Father, full of grace and truth"* (John 1:14).

> *"And without controversy great is the mystery of godliness: God was manifest in the flesh"* (1 Tim. 3:16).

> *"Forasmuch then as the children are partakers of flesh and blood, He also Himself likewise took part of the same; that through death he might destroy him that had the power of death, that is, the devil; And deliver them who through fear of death were all their lifetime subject to bondage"* (Heb. 2:14).

There are so many other Scriptures that present to us this wonderful fact! Search them out to your own blessing.

When they examined this amazing food, the children of Israel called it "Manna", which means "What is it?", for as the text says *"they wist not what it was"* (16:15). In relation to the Lord Jesus Christ, it speaks of the mystery of His humanity. At His birth, wise men and shepherds alike fell at His feet to worship Him. When in the temple at the age of twelve, He was listening to the doctors and asking them questions, *"And all that heard Him were astonished at His understanding and answers"* (Luke 2:47). On the stormy lake, the disciples experienced His magnificent power, when He rebuked the winds and the raging sea. They said one to another, *"What manner of man is this! For He commandeth even the winds and water, and they obey Him"* (Luke 8:25). When the officers came to take Him by force, they left without Him. Going back to the chief priests and Pharisees they said, *"Never man spake like this man"* (John 7:46). This was no ordinary man; He was God incarnate.

However, while He was unique, He was nevertheless a real man. He subjected Himself to the limitations of a human body. How can we understand what it meant for Him to be wearied with His journey by sitting on a well (John 4:6), or to sleep in a boat during a raging storm (Matt. 8:24), or to lie prostrate with his face to the ground in prayer (Matt. 26:39), or to weep at a graveside (John 11:35)? He entered into the various aspects of human life, yet He was without sin. Now as our great High Priest, He understands all that we are passing through. At God's right hand today, He is able to provide comfort and give strength to His people in their time of need (Heb. 4:14-16).

Another interesting aspect of this bread from heaven was its size. It seemed so small to their eyes as they gazed upon it with wonder! This speaks to us about our Lord's humility. The true and living bread that came to us, was of little significance as far as this world was concerned. *"He was in the world, and the world was made by Him, and the world knew Him not. He came to His own and His own received Him not"* (John 1:10-11). They said about Him, *"Is not this the carpenter's son?"* (Matt. 13:55). There was no outward majesty that radiated from Him. In spite of artists' impressions, there was no halo around His head. He appeared to be an ordinary man. Pilate asked Him, *"Art Thou a king then?"* To which our Lord replied, *"Thou sayest I am a king. To this end was I born, and for this cause came I into this world, that I should bear witness unto the truth. Every one that is of the truth heareth my voice"* (John 18:37). The attitude of the religious leaders was seen when they shouted, *"Crucify Him, crucify Him"* (John 19:6). Tragically, they placed no value upon the Son of God! It is beyond our comprehension *"that He made Himself of no reputation, and took on Him the form of a servant, and was made in the likeness of men: and being found in fashion as a man, He humbled Himself, and became obedient unto death, even the death of the cross"* (Phil. 2:7-8).

We are also told about the colour of the manna. The small, round bread was white, bringing before us the sinlessness of the Saviour. He was absolutely pure, internally and externally. *"For such an high priest became us, who is holy, harmless, undefiled, separate from sinners, and made higher than the heavens"* (Heb. 7:26). Peter says of Him, *"Who did no sin, neither was guile found in His mouth"* (1 Pet. 2:22). There was no other who caused the heavens to open and a voice to proclaim, *"Thou art my beloved Son, in whom I am well pleased"* (Mark 1:11). Who alone but the Lord Jesus Christ could say, *"Which of you convinceth me of sin?"* (John 8:46).

Finally, let us observe that the supply of this heavenly bread lasted for 40 years. It met their need, day by day, for the whole journey. This would bring us to appreciate our Lord's sufficiency. There is in Him all things to meet our every need, until He takes us home to heaven. When the children of Israel crossed over the Jordan, the manna ceased and they ate the corn of the promised land. This speaks of the Lord Jesus Christ in glory, who we will be with for all eternity.

When the bread had fallen, the people had to gather it, measure it, and bake it—before eating it! God provided it, but their responsibility was to gather a fresh portion for each day. Today, we have the written Word of God and, for us to be fed by it, we need to read, meditate, study and apply it on a daily basis. We can only come to know the Living Word of God more intimately when we spend time in the written Word of God. Go on to learn more of your wonderful Saviour, and seek to live for Him until He comes again.

12

WATER FROM THE ROCK

After the people were fed and rested, they started off again on their journey. In Exodus 17 their journey took them from the wilderness of Sin to Rephidim where they put up their tents. Soon they discovered there was no water for them to drink. Once more they lapsed into the attitude of murmuring and complaining. It would seem that Moses' patience was starting to run out with them. So he challenged them, saying, *"Why do you contend with me? Why do you tempt the Lord?"* In spite of all the people had experienced, they still showed a lack of trust as to why they had been delivered. *"Why is it you have brought us out of Egypt, to kill us and our children and our livestock with thirst?"* (NKJV). Moses, instead of taking action against them, wisely brought the issue to the Lord. He had learned that when things spin out of control, the best thing to do was to take it to the Lord in prayer. When situations overwhelm us, there is no better place to go than to the Lord. How true are the words of Joseph Scriven:

> What a Friend we have in Jesus,
> All our sins and griefs to bear!
> What a privilege to carry
> Everything to God in prayer!
> O what peace we often forfeit,
> O what needless pain we bear,
> All because we do not carry
> Everything to God in prayer!

It is no surprise that Moses received clear direction from

the Lord as to what to do next. *"Go on before the people."* The Lord reminded Moses of his responsibility in leading the flock of Israel. A true shepherd always goes on in front of the sheep. "The sheep hear his voice and follow him." Secondly, *"Take with you some of the elders of Israel"* (v. 5). He was not to be alone when he was addressing the situation to resolve it. What a good lesson for the elders of the assembly. They should always act together and not leave matters to one man.

Thirdly, *"Also take in your hand your rod with which you smote the river"* (v. 5). There must have been an air of anticipation in Moses' heart, for he knew what this meant from past experience. Also, the Lord said to him, *"Behold, I will stand before you there on the rock in Horeb; and you shall strike the rock, and water will come out of it, that the people may drink."* With great confidence, Moses did what the Lord asked him to do, and a great blessing came to the people that day!

Now to consider some of the spiritual truth represented in this historical event. We read in 1 Corinthians 10:4, *"They all drank the same spiritual drink, for they drank of that spiritual Rock that followed them, and that Rock was Christ."* He is the only source of all spiritual refreshment. David understood this and applied it to his life. He said, *"The Lord is my rock and my salvation"* (Ps. 18:2). The woman who met the Saviour in John 4:14 received the living water He was able to give her. *"But whosoever drinketh of the water that I shall give him shall never thirst; but the water that I shall give him shall be in him a well of water springing up into everlasting life."* Have you drunk from this source? Have you received this water of life that can truly satisfy?

> I tried the broken cisterns, Lord,
> But, ah! the waters failed!
> Ee'en as I stooped to drink they'd fled,
> And mocked me as I wailed.
> Now none but Christ can satisfy,
> None other name for me;
> There's love and life and lasting joy,
> Lord Jesus, found in thee.
>
> —B. E.

Having considered the **satisfying rock** (Ex. 17), which views the Lord Jesus Christ as the fountain of living water, let us see some other aspects throughout Scripture of Christ as a Rock.

In Isaiah 32:2 we read, *"And a man shall be as an hiding place from the wind, and a covert from the tempest; as rivers of water in a dry place, as the shadow of a great rock in a weary land."* Here we have a **sheltering rock** which provides a fortress to all who take cover under it. King Solomon looked upon four little things upon the earth that were exceeding wise and said of one of them, *"The conies are but a feeble folk, yet they make their houses in the rocks"* (Prov. 30:26). They were safe from all the storms that raged and were protected from every wind that blew. In our Lord Jesus Christ there is safety and shelter when all the storms of life blow. He is a place of refuge from the judgments to come.

Mighty tides about me sweep,
Perils lurk within the deep,
Angry clouds o'ershade the sky,
And the tempest rises high;
Still I stand the tempest's shock,
For my anchor grips the Rock.
—W. C. Martin

In the New Testament we read of the Lord Jesus' conclusion to His Sermon on the Mount in these words,

> *"Therefore whoever hears these sayings of Mine, and does them, I will liken him to a wise man who built his house on the rock: and the rain descended, the floods came, and the winds blew and beat on that house; and it did not fall, for it was founded on the rock.*
>
> *But everyone who hears these sayings of Mine, and does not do them, will be like a foolish man who built his house on the sand: and the rain descended, the floods came, and the winds blew and beat on that house; and it fell. And great was its fall"* (Matt. 7:24-27).

Here we have the **solid rock** which is the basis for a good foundation. What a great contrast to the foundation that is on sand. Both houses, from the outside, looked solid and probably drew a lot of attention. However, the lasting value was dependant upon its foundation—how secure it was! Paul says, *"According to the grace of God which is given unto me, as a wise masterbuilder, I have laid the foundation, and another buildeth thereon. But let every man take heed how he buildeth thereupon. For other foundation can no man lay than that is laid, which is Jesus Christ"* (1 Cor. 3:10-11). Is your foundation solid?

My hope is built on nothing less
Than Jesus blood and righteousness;
I dare not trust the sweetest frame,
But wholly lean on Jesus' name.
On Christ, the solid Rock, I stand;
All other ground is sinking sand.
—Edward Mote

As we move on from this remarkable day in Israel's history we must never forget that before the people's thirst was quenched, the rock had to be smitten! Before our Lord could provide us with living water and eternal life, He also had to be smitten! *"Surely He has borne our griefs and carried our sorrows yet we did esteem Him stricken, smitten by GOD, and afflicted"* (Isa. 53:4). All the benefits of Christ as our rock can only be ours because of what He suffered on the cross at Calvary. Take another look at what He has done!

13

THE ENEMY ATTACKS

Once more the people have seen their God provide wonderfully and meet all their needs. After the water flowed from the smitten rock they must have sung the Lord's song again. Each stage of the journey brought new and exciting experiences for them to sing about. However, as this multitude marched forward they did not realize that a powerful enemy was lurking around the corner. It was not the time to sit back and rest on their blessings. After all, they were still in the wilderness, not the Promised Land.

"Now Amalek came and fought with Israel in Rephidim" (Ex. 17:8). There would be many enemies for Israel to face. It is helpful to study these battles and apply the lessons to the spiritual battles we face. The various enemies give different lessons for handling different problems. Amalek was an enemy that came and attacked, so Israel had to stand up and fight. Others they had to flee from!

In considering this enemy, it is helpful to trace where Amalek came from and what were the defining characteristics. of this nation It is always wise to study carefully the place something is first mentioned in the Bible. In this case we can get to the root of this nation's attitudes. Likewise, we are able to learn some spiritual lessons from it.

We read in Genesis 36:12, *"And Timna was concubine to Eliphaz Esau's son; and she bare to Eliphaz Amalek: these* [were] *the sons of Adah Esau's wife."* From this verse we discover that the Amalakites were the descendants of Esau. The description given of Esau in Genesis 25:27 says, *"Esau was a skillful hunter, a man of the field."* His great passion in life was killing to feed his own fleshly desires. One day, coming in from the field, he was weary having caught nothing. *"And Esau said to Jacob, Feed me, I pray thee, with that same red pottage; for I am faint: therefore was his name called Edom. And Jacob said, Sell me this day thy birthright. And Esau said, Behold, I am at the point to die: and what profit shall this birthright do to me?"* (Gen. 25:30-32). So Jacob gave him bread and stew and in this way *"Esau despised his birthright!"* (v. 34).

The writer in Hebrews 12:16-17 sums up this incident by calling Esau a *"fornicator, who for one morsel of food sold his birthright. For you know that afterward, when he wanted to inherit the blessing, he was rejected, for he found no place for repentance, though he sought it diligently with tears"* (NKJV). The first thing we learn about this formidable enemy of Israel was that they descended from one who rejected the title deeds to the blessings of God and pursued his own natural desires—desires of the flesh and mind. What a high price Esau paid for putting more value on the material and temporal rather than on spiritual and eternal things. Where does your interest lie today? The Lord Jesus says, *"For where your treasure is, there your heart will be also"* (Matt. 6:21 NKJV).

Another characteristic of the Amalakites is found in Deuteronomy 25:17-18: *"Remember what Amalek did to you on the way as you were coming out of Egypt, how he met you on the way and attacked your rear ranks, all the stragglers at your rear, when you were tired and weary; and he did not fear God."* In other words, Amalek attacked those who were on the outskirts of the tribes. The most dangerous place for the believer to be is following the Lord at a distance. Peter was caught off guard when, instead of being in the forefront, he *"stood at the door outside"* (John 18:16). What followed was his denial of his Lord—words which later caused him deep sorrow and heartache. Are you living a shallow kind of spiritual life, trying not to be too committed to the things of God? You are an easy prey for a satanic attack, which could well bring spiritual disaster.

Considering this incident further, we see that the Amalakites went after the weak and weary. Paul lays great emphasis in Romans 14:1 about receiving those who are weak in the faith. In 15:1 he says, *"We then that are strong ought to bear the infirmities of the weak, and not to please ourselves."* This is so important to do, lest the weak be attacked and devoured by the fleshly influences that surround them. John says, *"I write unto you, young men, because you are strong, and the word of God abides in you"* (1 Jn. 2:14 NKJV). Here is the only way to protect ourselves from the activity of the flesh in our lives. There is no substitute for daily reading and meditation on the Word of God. It not only makes us strong, but it protects us from the fiery darts of the evil one. The Lord Jesus says on one occasion, *"Men ought always to pray and not to faint"*—and not lose heart (Luke 18:1). One of the best remedies for weary hearts is prayer. This is another safeguard for the heart when the flesh rises up to struggle against the spirit. We have this great resource available at all times—access to the Father in every time of need. Keep close to God!

Later in Israel's experience, King Saul was commanded by the Lord of Hosts to attack Amalek and utterly destroy all they had. He was ordered to kill man and woman, infant and nursing child, ox and sheep, camel and donkey (1 Sam. 15:3). However, when asked why he did not fulfill his mission, he said, *"But, I have obeyed the voice of the Lord, and gone on the mission on which the Lord sent me, and brought back Agag King of Amalek; I have utterly destroyed the Amalakites. But the people took of the plunder, sheep and oxen, the best of the things which should have been utterly destroyed, to sacrifice to the Lord your God in Gilgal"* (1 Sam. 15:20-21). What a stern rebuke he received from Samuel! *"Has the Lord as great delight in burnt offerings and sacrifices, as in obeying the Lord? Behold, to obey is better than sacrifice, and to heed than the fat of rams"* (v. 22). Saul paid a great price for his disobedience—he lost his position as King of Israel. Amalek was a relentless foe that should have been utterly destroyed.

Unfortunately, some were spared to continue to harass and war against God's people in years to come.

These lessons are paralleled in the New Testament. Amalek speaks of the flesh, which is the old nature in action. Paul says in Romans 3:20 *"Therefore by the deeds of the law no flesh will be justified."* Nothing that is done in the energy of our old Adamic nature can ever be justified before God. But still so many are trying their best to win God's favor. This, however, is completely insufficient. Neither can the believer win God's approval, *"For those who live according to the flesh set their minds on the things of the flesh, but those who live according to the Spirit, the things of the Spirit. ... So then, those who are in the flesh cannot please God"* (Rom. 8:5-8).

Paul was greatly disturbed by the conditions of the Corinthian church. There were divisions among them because they held certain men in admiration. Paul, Apollos and Peter had become the objects of special followings within the church. This was the result of carnal and fleshly attitudes in the believers. In dealing with this issue Paul directs them to the wisdom of God as seen in the preaching of the cross. This puts an end to all that is of Adam, crucifying the old man with its lusts. He sums up by saying, *"That no flesh should glory in his presence. But of him are ye in Christ Jesus, who of God is made unto us wisdom, and righteousness, and sanctification, and redemption: That, according as it is written, He that glorieth, let him glory in the Lord"* (1 Cor. 1:29-31). It is evident then that there is nothing good said about the flesh and its activity. It constantly wages war against the Spirit. *"Walk in the Spirit and you shall not fulfill the lust of the flesh. For the flesh lusts against the Spirit; ... and these are contrary to one another* (Gal. 5:16-17).

When Paul spoke of his natural qualifications, he said, *"If anyone else thinks he may have confidence in the flesh, I more so: circumcised the eighth day, of the stock of Israel, of the tribe of Benjamin, a Hebrew of the Hebrews; concerning the law, a Pharisee; concerning zeal, persecuting the church; concerning the righteousness which is in the law, blameless"* (Phil. 3:4-6 NKJV). What a pedigree! Here was a young man who had much to boast about.

He had everything going for him. He was climbing the social, religious and political ladders! Being influential, he used his authority to get what he wanted. However, at the height of it all, while still pursuing his natural desires, he met the Risen Saviour! Looking back on his life he said, *"But what things were gain to me, these I have counted loss for Christ, Yet indeed I count all things loss for the excellence of the knowledge of Christ Jesus my Lord, for whom I have suffered the loss of all things, and count them as rubbish that I may gain Christ"* (Phil. 3:7-8).

This is deeply challenging, isn't it? Paul gives a practical warning in Romans 13:14: *"But put on the Lord Jesus Christ, and make no provision for the flesh, to fulfill its lusts."* Do not give any room for the desires of the flesh in its many different guises. Deal with your fleshly desires before they ultimately destroy your spiritual life.

Returning to the scene in Exodus 17, we see that Israel was victorious over Amalek in battle. Moses, Aaron and Hur climbed the hill, while the battle between the Amalakites and Israelites raged in the valley below. *"And so it was, when Moses held up his hand, that Israel prevailed; and when he let down his hand, Amalek prevailed"* (Ex. 17:11). It was the man up on the mountain who made the difference. And when Moses grew weary, Aaron and Hur kept his hands in the air. What a great victory was won in this unique way. This reminds us that today, we have our Man on high, interceding for us who are in the valley below. *"For we do not have a High Priest who cannot sympathize with our weaknesses, but was in all points tempted as we are, yet without sin. Let us therefore come boldly to the throne of grace that we may obtain mercy and find grace, to help in time of need"* (Heb. 4:15-16). We keep looking, not to uplifted hands but to an uplifted Saviour at God's right hand.

Through manifold temptation,
My soul holds on its course;
Christ's mighty intercession,
Alone is my resource.
My gracious high priest's pleadings,
Who on the cross did bleed,
Bring down God's grace and blessings,
Help in each hour of need.
— A. P. Cecil

14

THE LAW WAS GIVEN

With victory achieved at Rephidim, they came to the next stopping place, *"the mountain of God"* (Ex. 18:5). It was now the third month since they had left Egypt. *"For they were departed from Rephidim, and were come [to] the desert of Sinai, and had pitched in the wilderness; and there Israel camped before the mount"* (Ex. 19:2). It is here that two of the most important events in the history of the nation of Israel took place. The narrative shifts its emphasis away from the journey and onto God's purposes for His people. Now, the real reason He brought them out of Egypt was unfolded to them. God was preparing the way in which He could dwell among them.

In chapter eighteen we gain an insight into the tremendous load Moses was carrying as he dealt with the many issues between the people. From morning to evening Moses listened to their various needs, and he was handling them all by himself. His father-in-law observed what was happening and said to him, *"The thing you do is not good. Both you and these people who are with you will surely wear yourselves out. For this thing is too much for you, you are not able to perform it by yourself"* (Ex. 18:17-18 NKJV). Jethro's advice to Moses was to appoint able men who feared God, men of truth, and men who hated covetousness, to be judges over the people. The most serious matters Moses would handle himself. We see the humble spirit of Moses for he *"heeded the voice of his father in law and did all that he had said"* (Ex. 18:24). It is for the younger to heed and respect the older. The voice of experience should never be despised!

The mountain they had now come to was where God was going to make known His laws for Israel to follow. Before God communicated with them, He set boundaries so that they would not come near the mountain. If they came near, they would die. It was here that the divine standards of holiness were revealed in what we call the Ten Commandments. Of course, in reading over these chapters, we realize that there were more than ten requirements for them to live by. As you take time to read through chapters nineteen to twenty four, you will get insight into what was expected from them. There were moral, social, religious and ethical responsibilities to be observered. There were many details of ceremony and rituals for the chosen race to follow.

From whatever angle we examine these laws it is clear that they were God's holy law and He demanded absolute and complete obedience. This was not something optional. It was to be taken very seriously. Whenever we consider Mount Sinai, we are reminded of the condemnation of sin. No Israelite would ever forget the awesome sight of a mountain cloaked in thick cloud, the incessant flash of lightning, the constant rumble of thunder, and the sound of a very loud trumpet. When the Lord descended upon the mountain in fire the smoke was like the smoke of a furnace, and the mountain quaked. Such was the effect on the people that they trembled and stood afar off. It was from this awe inspiring scene that God spoke, and Moses wrote all the words the Lord had spoken. How re-assuring it is for us, *"For you have not come to the mountain that may be touched and that burned with fire, and to blackness and darkness and tempest, and the sound of a trumpet and the voice of words, so that those who heard it begged that the word should not be spoken to them any more"* (Heb. 12:18 NKJV). One of the great blessings of our salvation is that we are free from the Law and from its penalty.

It is helpful to look at the law as viewed in the New Testament Scriptures. Romans 3:19-20 says *"Now we know that whatever the law says, it says to those who are under the law, that every mouth may be stopped, and all the world may become guilty before*

God. Therefore by the deeds of the law no flesh will be justified in His sight, for by the law is the knowledge of sin." What a sad judgment against the human race! To sum it up, *"all have sinned and come short of the glory of God"* (Rom. 3:23). The law showed how utterly impossible it was for fallen man to please God. So, the law was a law of condemnation. Whether one were Jew or Gentile, the whole world was guilty and at the mercy of God.

This law that condemned and brought a guilty verdict was in itself unable to save or rescue the sinner. In Romans 8:3 we learn, *"What the law could not do in that it was weak through the flesh, God did by sending His own Son in the likeness of sinful flesh, on account of sin: He condemned sin in the flesh"* (NKJV). But what the law was unable to do, the Son of God was able to fulfill. *"For the law of the Spirit of life in Christ Jesus has made me free from the law of sin and death"* (Rom. 8:2 NKJV).

Free from the law O happy condition,
Jesus hath bled and there is remission;
Cursed by the law and bruised by the fall,
Grace hath redeemed us once for all.
—P. P. Bliss

In the epistle to the Galatians, our relationship to the law is spelled out. It is seen as, *"our schoolmaster to bring us to Christ that we might be justified by faith"* (Gal. 3:24). This is an interesting illustration, for it shows us that the law has many things to teach us in its school. We are taught that the law had many good elements; that it was just and holy. However, its real purpose was to bring us to the Lord Jesus Christ. A true relationship to God could only be found by faith in Christ. *"But after that faith is come, we are no longer under a schoolmaster. For ye are all the children of God by faith in Christ Jesus"* (Gal. 3:25-26). Are you still trying to keep the law? Or are you resting completely in the Lord?

The writer in Hebrews 10:1 tells us, *"For the law, having a shadow of the good things to come, and not the very image of the things, can never with these same sacrifices, which they offer continually year by year, make those who approach perfect."* How totally inadequate was the law and its sacrifices to deal with sin. All those ceremonies and rituals from the past could not give peace to any guilty conscience. Those sacrifices could not take away one single sin, or remove one single stain. This desperate condition of mankind would have presented a very gloomy, hopeless outlook indeed if that had been the end of the story. But the writer goes on to say, *"every priest stands ministering daily and offering repeatedly the same sacrifices, which can never take away sins. But this Man, after He had offered one sacrifice for sins forever, sat down at the right hand of God"* (Heb. 10:11-12).

My faith has found a resting place,
Not in device nor creed;
I trust the Ever-living One,
His wounds for me shall plead.
I need no other argument,
I need no other plea,
It is enough that Jesus died,
And that He died for me.
—Lidie H. Edmunds

Having come to this appreciation of deliverance from the penalty of the law through faith in Christ, Paul addresses a disturbing issue in his letter to Timothy. In 1 Timothy 1:6 he writes that, *"some having strayed, have turned aside to idle talk, Desiring to be teachers of the law, understanding neither what they say nor the things which they affirm."* These men were still trying to teach the old Judaism. They were returning again to the school masters, going back to what they had left! Paul reminds them that the law had a purpose and standard for living, but our relationship to the law has changed. Now he says, *"If there is any other thing contrary to sound doctrine, according to the glorious gospel of the blessed God which was committed to my trust"* (vv. 10-11). Here he establishes a completely new standard for living. The gospel gives us a new nature whereby we are able to live lives that uphold the law. The gospel not only saves but it changes and makes good citizens of us. We now have a divine power giving us *"all things that pertain unto life and godliness"* (2 Pet. 1:3).

But at Mount Sinai God made Himself known in a fearsome way. What He had given to His people were laws, which if obeyed would bring blessing. However, any transgression of them would bring severe judgment. In this, God was also preparing them for life in the Promised Land. We now leave this section of travel through the wilderness, and to continue the journey, we need to turn to the Book of Numbers.

15

GOD'S DWELLING PLACE

The third section of the Book of Exodus covers 15 chapters. In it, we are not told any more about the journey through the wilderness. The story continues in the Book of Numbers with further accounts of all their encampments on the way to the Promised Land. At this juncture, the people are located close to Mount Sinai. Picture for the moment this beautiful scene where the tabernacle was constructed. When Balaam came to curse the children of Israel he said, *"How goodly are thy tents, O Jacob, and thy tabernacles, O Israel"* (Num. 24:5). It must have been a beautiful sight. How could he curse the people whom God had blessed?

Because the contents of these last chapters of Exodus are a subject by itself I will only make a few comments on them. There are some excellent books available on these chapters which would be worth adding to your library. However, let us consider some of the general aspects of truth related to what the tabernacle meant to the children of Israel. This is also profitable for our learning and instruction. In Romans 15:4 we read, *"For whatever things were written before were written for our learning, that we through the patience and comfort of the Scriptures might have hope."* There is a wealth of resources available to us in the Scriptures, giving guidance and direction for our spiritual walk and development.

The directions for the construction of the tabernacle were given by God Himself. *"And let them make Me a sanctuary; that*

I may dwell among them. According to all that I show you, after the pattern of the tabernacle" (Ex. 25:8-9). This is repeated again in 26:30; 27:8; Numbers 8:4; Acts 7:44; and Hebrews 8:5. We must never forget that the architect and designer was God. Moses, the recipient of this unique and amazing blueprint, had to make it exactly as he was told. This meant that no human thought or idea could be interjected into this building. Moses could not consult Aaron, the priests, or the people as to what they thought it should look like. This was God's plan and everything connected to it had a divine purpose.

What lessons can we learn from this, in relation to the things of God? In an age when modern philosophy and human intellect has sought to tear apart the Word of God, we need to be careful we do not join in. There is no greater danger than worldly reasoning creeping in, seeking to distort and destroy divine revelation. Beware of anyone, no matter who they are, who seeks to give you his own private interpretation of Scripture. How often we hear of ideas or further communications from God. This is an age when most people want to hear something new. The more bizarre the interpretations, the more readily acceptable they seem to become.

This blueprint of the tabernacle was not for Moses' private use. It was a communication for every one who belongs to the Lord. God does not do anything in secret. He makes His will known to all. The newborn babe in Christ has access to the whole counsel of God as much as the mature and gifted believer. The person to whom God chooses to communicate His truth does not become the owner of it. Therefore, let us come in true submission to the authority of the Word of God in our lives, and share His truth with one another.

It is important to notice the place where this pattern was given to Moses. This is the same place the Law of God had been given previously, where there was great darkness, thunder, and lightening so the people could not draw near. What a contrast, as God now shows to Moses a way whereby His people could draw near to Him. It was His desire to dwell among His people. This was the very purpose for which He brought them out of Egypt. What wonderful experiences throughout the Word of God took place upon the top of mountains! Take time to use your concordance and trace them through Scripture and you will have a wonderful study. *"And Moses went up to the mount, and a cloud covered the mount. And the glory of the Lord abode upon mount Sinai"* (Ex. 24:15-16).

God unfolded His great design to Moses, wrapped in His own divine glory. The ultimate purpose of God is to use everything to glorify Himself. Every action that reveals God's character brings honour and glory to Him. O, that we may appreciate why He saved us. It will only be in eternity that we will be able to fully understand His wisdom in it all. Every creature will bring glory to Him. However, His desire is that this glory should come from redeemed hearts. They will, out of deep love, and through the riches of His grace, sing His praises forever and ever. Have we begun that song now so that by our lips and by our lives we glorify Him?

This unique plan provided the people a new way to approach God. They had never experienced anything like it before. The tabernacle was erected so Israel might function as a holy and royal priesthood. This meant that the family chosen from the sons of Levi would act as priests on behalf of the people before God. Here is another wonderful sphere of truth to enjoy when you look at it through the New Testament in the book of Hebrews. It is worthwhile to study the similarities and distinctions between Aaron and our Lord Jesus Christ as High Priests. You will find it spiritually profitable.

16

FINAL COMMENTS

We have considered the importance of the tabernacle being built in accordance with the pattern shown on the mount. Notice also its position—the middle of the camp. It was to be erected right in the centre of God's people. All the tribes with their families erected their tents surrounding the tabernacle. As previously mentioned these people could not be cursed when God was at their centre. The picture presented in the tabernacle reveals truth to us in three different ways. Firstly and primarily, it speaks of the Lord Jesus Christ. In John 1:14 we read, *"And the word became flesh and dwelt* (or tabernacled) *amongst us and we beheld His glory, the glory as of the only begotten of the Father."* He came right into the centre of our world. Paul says, *"And without controversy great is the mystery of godliness: God was manifested in the flesh"* (1 Tim. 3:16). Those wonderful words expressed by the angel in Matthew 1:23 say *"Behold a virgin shall be with child and bear a Son, and they shall call His name Immanuel, which translated is, 'God with us'."* Deity clothed Himself with humanity, and came down to dwell with men. But men rejected and crucified Him. However, God raised Him from the dead and He has been exalted and made very high. If you have received Him as Saviour and Lord by faith, are you giving Him the central place in your life? It is the right thing to do for He has done so much for you by His death on the cross.

Secondly, the tabernacle is a picture of the church. Stephen, in his address to the nation of Israel in Acts 7:38, spoke of the tabernacle as the church in the wilderness. The tabernacle was the centre of gathering! In like manner our Lord Jesus Christ is the centre of our gathering today. In 1 Corinthians 1:2, Paul says, *"Unto the church of God which is at Corinth, to them that are sanctified in Christ Jesus, called to be saints, with all that in every place call upon the name of Jesus Christ our Lord, both theirs and ours."* They did not gather to a special preacher, orator, or Bible teacher, nor to any man-made programs or ideas. There is something so beautiful and simple when we gather to the Person who died and rose again for us! For the church at Laodicea (Rev. 3:14-22) everything was going so well. It was rich, had plenty of goods, and did not need anything. They were so self-sufficient, but the Lord Jesus was on the outside knocking for admission. He had been displaced from the centre of gathering. Many churches today seem to have it all together except that the Lord is not in the midst. Are you fellowshipping with those who are gathered in His Name?

Thirdly, it is good to give some thought to the provisions and materials of the tabernacle. The materials used in the construction of the tabernacle were given by free will offerings (Ex. 25:2). These gifts had been brought out of Egypt and they were freely handed over at the request of God. It was seen as an opportunity to give something to God for all that He had done for them. Remember, these materials were received from the Egyptians. We too need to realize that what we receive is directly given due to the benevolent care of the Creator. What have you given in return for all that the Lord has done for you? Exercise your heart to meet the need of someone you know who could benefit from it. With what attitude do you give to the Lord? Is it as He requested, giving out of an exercised heart for the benefit of the Lord's work.

There were various types of materials used for different functions. Metals—gold, silver, brass. Curtains—blue, scarlet, purple, fine linen. Coverings—goat's hair, ram's and badger's skins. Wood—acacia. Minerals—oil. Spices—stacte, onycha, galbanum, frankincense. Stones—sardus, topaz, carbuncle, emerald, sapphire, diamond, ligure, agate, amethyst, beryl, onyx and jasper! There is a treasury of divine truth represented by these materials. As this will take another volume to cover, I will leave it for you to take your concordance and search out their meanings and lessons. There are some excellent books on the tabernacle.

Finally what is the purpose and meaning of the tabernacle? The writer to the Hebrews presents some truths regarding its significance. In Hebrews 8:5, we read it is a *"shadow of heavenly things."* In 9:1, it is called *"an earthly sanctuary."* The word sanctuary means a "clean place". In 9:6 we are told that it *"accomplishes the service of God."* All the work within the tabernacle was done by priestly service. In 9:9 it is a figure for the time then present. This means that it had a specific ministry to the children of Israel. In 9:23 it is *"a pattern of things in the heavens."* God has given us a little glimpse of His glory in this earthly structure. When the earthly has truly vanished away heaven will be realized in all its infinite fullness. The tabernacle picture has now gone and we are waiting for the upward call to the realms of glory.

In summary, the tabernacle brings to a climax what God intended for His people. There are three things most significant concerning this temporary tent in the wilderness. It was the place where God dwelt in the midst of His people. Secondly, it was the place where God's people worshipped Him. Thirdly, it was a place of revelation about God and heavenly realities. Now, when we consider a New Testament church, these three elements should also be seen. Is your local assembly giving the Lord His true place in the centre? Does the local church function as the channel through which God is worshipped? Is the assembly active in effective outreach with the glorious Gospel of our Lord Jesus Christ? As you continue in your studies of this very important subject, may the Holy Spirit enlighten to you the deep truths of God's Word. I trust you will apply the practical challenges presented here to your heart and that you will live for the Lord Jesus Christ today and every day until He returns.

Printed in the United States
206609BV00001B/61-84/A